Spicing Up Married Life

Satisfying Couples' Hunger for True Love

Fr. Leo Patalinghug

LMcW
Films

Hunt Valley, MD

Published in the United States by
Renegade Productions, Inc., Hunt Valley, MD
www.renegadecommunications.com

ISBN 978-0-9796035-3-2

Printed in the United States of America

For more information about Grace Before Meals go to
www.GraceBeforeMeals.com

Dedicated to:

My loving parents Carlos and Fe
on the occasion of their 50th Wedding Anniversary

Acknowledgements:

Prayerful thanks goes to so many people who helped put this book in your hands. First and foremost, I thank my family—my parents, siblings, in-laws, nieces, and nephews—for their encouragement, support, and love. My faithful (not perfect) family teaches me to receive and share God's merciful love. I pray that couples engage the information in this book and use these recipe suggestions to help strengthen their love for each other and their family.

I want to thank the dedicated staff at Renegade Productions who worked long hours putting this book together in its final form. In particular, I want to thank my good friend Tim Watkins, President and CEO, as well as his wonderful family. Sincere thanks go to the Project Manager Joe Hansbrough for his dedication and faithful example as a new husband and father; Graphic Designer William Phillips for making pictures look so beautiful; Louise Cooper who served as the (much-needed) proofreader; John Newton who designed the cover and chapter layouts with artistic flare; and Louie Verrecchio as the Chief Editor who helped bring clarity to my words and ideas in each chapter.

Along with the Grace Before Meals team, I used the photography expertise of Kevin Maher of Seven Set Studios. I also thank John Buechsenstein of the Culinary Institute of America in Napa Valley for offering sommelier expertise by pairing delicious beverages with each meal. For information on how to find these pairings, go to www.gracebeforemeals.com.

I also relied on the prayers and examples of many people in my extended church family, from the encouragement of the Church leadership, to my brother priests and the parishioner couples who have given great example of faithfulness and love.

In response to our Internet and social media outreach, we were pleased to have so many people apply to be recipe-testers for this book. After reading about people's stories and learning about their cooking skill level, we handpicked a very special group of people! We were edified by the support of these official recipe-testers, including: Joe and Erica Hansbrough, Martin and Amanda Braniff, Steve and Mikayla Dalton, Chad and Chandra Law, Bernie and Vickie Laubner, Dustin and Allicia Faber, Gordon and Amy Laque, Josh and Mathilda Mellon, Jeff and Susan Bertram, Joe and Ciera Osipenko, Owen and Carrie Harkey, Steve Drennen and Elizabeth Jalandoni, Jason and Cindi Bond, Timothy and Julie Huisken, David and Lulu Thayer, and of course, so many other family and friends who taste-tested my cooking over the years (and cleaned up the dishes). The responses from these recipe-testers prove that cooking a deliciously romantic meal—even for the non-expert cooks—is helpful in establishing a stronger relationship with each other. To quote one of the recipe testers, "It was a fantastic afternoon spent together as a couple, focused only on serving each other. What a beautiful gift."

May this book bring a special blessing to your relationship! I firmly believe that inviting God to each of your monthly anniversary meals brings grace to your dinner, meaning to your love, and spice to your married life!

Fr. Leo Patalinghug

Setting the Table
What's in This Book?

Grace Before Meals

Spicing Up Married Life!

Written by: Rev. Leo E. Patalinghug STL

Spousal love helps determine the strength of family bonds. I've seen it, and I believe it!

While it may seem strange for an unmarried priest to write a book about marriage (much less a cookbook about marriage), I know that God calls His priests "spouses to the Bride of Christ—the Church" to help answer some of the difficult questions that couples often have. The Lord grants the pastors of His Church the privileged task of helping husbands and wives rekindle the Godly love they share at all stages of married life. To that end, He has entrusted the fullness of truth about loving marriages to His Church!

I've spent many years preparing couples for marriage. I have taught future priests how to do the same. I've also led marriage and parent counseling sessions and have had the pleasure of celebrating anniversaries with many faithful and loving couples who put Christ's simple command into practice: to love one another as He loves us!

While most popular wedding destinations don't require a priest, we know that Las Vegas-style-wedding-chapel marriages don't have anywhere near the track record of Sacramental wedding ceremonies witnessed in the Church. No wonder so many couples are inspired to request a priest to be part of that great celebration on their wedding day!

Even though media pundits and judicial activists are busy trying to redefine marriage, many people still recognize that God, not the court system, is the author of marriage. They know

that He is the One who brings two people together, sometimes with the help of family, friends, or even a dating service. Perhaps that is why so many people still believe that the church's wedding bells help make that day more special, holy, memorable, and sacred.

The popular culture's views, paired with rising statistics for both separation and divorce, don't paint a very encouraging picture of marriage. The Church, however, provides a long line of witnesses who are uniquely qualified to teach couples the true meaning of marriage, as well as to provide them with guidance on how to develop a long-lasting, loving relationship. As the author of marriage, God sustains the marital bond and gives the Church the sacraments to nurture and strengthen spouses, helping them with the grace they need to keep the promises they have made to one another.

If spouses depend only on one another to keep their marriage strong, they'll quickly discover that excluding God's love invites a struggle against powerful forces that can undermine their earthly commitment. Dependence upon God, however, strengthens the couple, aiding them in fulfilling their marriage vows. His wisdom teaches husbands and wives how to defend themselves against the spiritual attacks that challenge their resolve, and He imparts the theological virtue of hope that reminds spouses that their goal is to help one another get to Heaven, the wedding feast of all eternity!

Husbands and wives must remain aware that a good marriage is all about faithfulness, i.e., *being full of faith!* It's not just about the wedding gown, the reception, or the honeymoon. Unfortunately, this point often gets lost in the wedding plans.

In the midst of all the wedding preparations or the day-to-day grind of married life, not to mention the complacency that can sometimes set in after many years together, it's easy to forget that in marriage God offers us a glimpse, a foretaste of Heaven. (Did you catch the "food" reference—a fore-"taste"?)

It's important for married couples (especially as time goes by) to reflect upon those romantic feelings that were so plentiful in the early years and to remind themselves that God's love is dynamic, bringing new life, *eternal life,* to those who are faithful. Marriage is a blessing that comes from God. It is He who blesses it, upholds it, and creates within it a special place to infuse more love into the world.

As a Catholic priest, I offer this book about marriage and romantic meals as a gift to be shared by husbands and wives. Like my first book, *Recipes and Inspirations for Family Meals and Family Life,* this edition is much more than just a cookbook. It's a collection of ideas, ingredients, and recipes to help married couples, whether just starting out or celebrating a jubilee, to experience all of the blessings that God has in store for them as they grow in faith.

Using This Book

The Church and her pastors want to help you attain more of what you desire as a couple: a happy, holy, faithful commitment to God and one other. This book simply offers suggestions and guidance that will help strengthen what you already have in each other: God's love.

Each chapter contains several sections, the first of which is called *Listening Together.* In this section, couples (whether you are dating or celebrating a Golden Wedding Anniversary) are presented with a brief epigraph taken from Sacred Scripture or from the prayers that are part of the Ritual of Holy Matrimony.

The quotations found in *Listening Together* are intended to set the tone for the next section, *Learning Together*, which includes bite-sized theological essays that explore different aspects of marriage, breaking open and illuminating the vows that couples profess on their wedding day. (Did you get the other food reference: "bite-sized?" That means, couples can easily read this before their dinner date.)

As many counseling experts will attest, poor communication can contribute a great deal to a marriage's demise. This alone is motive enough for me to "stir the pot" a little bit, to get couples to "mix it up" themselves about the things that matter most. This brings us to *Talking Together.* In this section, spouses are given an opportunity to share in a conversion of heart through a variety of conversation topics. Here, couples will find discussion questions that are designed to prompt fun, faithful, lively, and at times, challenging dialogue.

This section ties directly into the *Grace Before Meals* philosophy, encouraging meaningful discussion around the dinner table. Talk about a great date!

From there, couples will be reminded of the value of *Praying Together*. In this section, couples will find a prayer based on the theme of the chapter that they may pray together, perhaps as the *grace after the meal.* After all, marriage requires a three-way conversation between man, woman, and God. Couples are encouraged to use either this prayer or another one of their choosing, be it from Sacred Scripture, a prayer book, or perhaps even one they write for themselves.

The point is simply *to pray together!* As couples progress through the book, they will come to discover why prayer is truly the best form of communication of all, since it invites God into the discussion.

Of course, we also need a section about food! *Dining Together* inspires spouses to go on an affordable, delicious, and romantic dinner date right in their very own kitchen. The suggested menus and recipes offer meal ideas that any couple can create together, no matter what their level of culinary talent.

Those who are familiar with the *Grace Before Meals* movement know that I like to encourage creativity in menu planning. I care far more about the process of eating together than the specifics of food preparation, seasoning, and presentation. It doesn't take an expensive study to show me that couples that take time to share a meal together have stronger relationships. My experience working with married people proves it, and it really shouldn't come as a surprise. After all, isn't that a big part of how your relationship grew when you were dating—a romantic picnic, coffee, dinner? Why stop that momentum after marriage?

So go ahead and use my menu suggestions and recipes, but feel free to change them up with other dishes or use your own creative cooking skills to spice up or tone down my suggestions. I'm proud to say that my recipes have been tested by married couples and have not only won their approval, but in some cases, have even become household favorites.

The final section, *Growing Together,* asks couples to commit to ongoing growth in love for one another by taking their own ideas, memories, and prayers and turning them into a resolution. We all need to have our hearts stirred with love the same way a pot needs a stir before it boils over or the way a familiar recipe might need a little "reinvention" to prevent monotony or boredom. In this section, couples will have an opportunity to bring each chapter to a close by writing down thoughts and ideas that will help them live out the words, "I do!"

While I wholeheartedly encourage spouses to celebrate their love for one another in a special way every single day, with our busy schedules, it helps to have a more realistic goal.

With a total of twelve chapters, this book provides couples with a ready-made game plan for celebrating their wedding day, not just one day a year, but *a dozen days a year!* A good idea might be to set aside the "day" of the wedding (e.g., the 10th of each month) or perhaps the weekend of the wedding (e.g., the second weekend of each month) as that special time specifically set aside to share a night of feasting, praying, and heartfelt conversation. Your marriage is important every day! So why wait an entire year to celebrate your anniversary?

As a Catholic priest, I may not have firsthand experience in marriage, but I do know that God has given His Catholic Church and her pastors the wisdom necessary to help couples stay strongly and passionately in love with each other. Ultimately, the *Grace Before Meals* movement wants to strengthen your marriage and your family the way God does, around His table. A loving table is an especially good way to satisfy our hunger, body, mind. and soul.

This particular *Grace Before Meals* book, however, has a rather specific objective: *to spice up your married life*, bringing a true blessing to your next dinner date as a couple married in God's love!

Remember, it was Jesus Himself who compared Heaven to an "eternal wedding banquet." This book doesn't attempt to reinvent that teaching; instead, it simply encourages husbands and wives to bring a little bit of Heaven's goodness to their marriage, both now and *'til death do you part.*

Chapter 1

Love At First Sight

Did You Find It?

> *Then I saw a new heaven and a new earth. The former heaven and the former earth had passed away, and the sea was no more. I also saw the holy city, a new Jerusalem, coming down out of heaven from God, prepared as a bride adorned for her husband.*
>
> REVELATION 21:1–2

Love at first sight! We read about it in fairy tales. It brings tears to our eyes when we're watching a good love story (which I affectionately call, "a mystery film"). After all, love is definitely mysterious, and like all good mysteries, we're captivated by these stories of romance until the mystery is solved, or in this case, when true love is finally discovered.

The desire for love at first sight makes people's eyes wander at bars, nightclubs, parties, and even religious services. They look here, there, and everywhere for that right person. They dress to impress, hoping to catch the eye of the perfect someone they're destined to meet. You may have noticed how some people can hold a conversation with one person, while paying attention to every other person that walks by. If someone of interest is spotted, the eyes often shift to the next most important body part: the ring finger.

A little ring on a particular finger determines whether to take the next step closer or to take steps in another direction. Just like the Israelites wandering 40 years in the desert, searching for the Promised Land flowing with milk and honey, people search for the one true love that God promises us.

The search for love can sometimes put a person's soul at risk. Unfortunately, some people "look for love in all the wrong places": smoky bars, lonely street corners or "anonymous" websites.

Given our culture's fast food mentality, some people think that finding true love should be as easy as ordering a burger and fries. Sadly, people sometimes treat dating and the search for love almost as casually as picking up a bite to eat at a drive thru: "Do you want brains with that blond hair and blue eyes? Or do you just want to supersize it?"

The incredible mystery of love deserves more attention, time, and energy than those who hold popularized misconceptions of love tend to give it. Just like any great mystery, finding love requires faith and patience. This is why a good love story is so much more than just a fairytale.

The desire for love—the kind that knocks your socks off when you first meet that special someone—can definitely motivate even the most spend-thrifty among us! Businesses know it, and they capitalize on it.

Have you ever seen those advertisements for professional dating services that promise anywhere from a 10-minute lunch conversation to a weeklong dating cruise? Matchmaking is a multi-million dollar industry. I suppose this explains the popularity of the 1970's hit television show, "The Love Boat." Well, almost!

A fear of being alone for the rest of their lives gives many people a sense of urgency, and even impatience, for finding that right person. Looking for love at first sight, however, isn't necessarily the best way to find everlasting love. Perhaps this investigation into the mystery of love requires a better understanding of the source of love.

First, I'm happy to tell you that love at first sight is possible; we just need to know where to look for it. Finding love doesn't begin with paying a dating service; it begins with paying attention to God—the ultimate matchmaker! If you don't believe me, just consider Adam and Eve, Sarah and Abraham, Anne and Joachim, Mary and Joseph, and of course, Jesus and His Bride—the Heavenly Jerusalem (aka, the Church, as we discovered in the Bible passage at the beginning of this chapter).

I'd say that God has a rather impressive track record of bringing together couples that were blessed with a long-lasting, loving relationship! It is safe to say that He really does know how to forge a "match made in Heaven."

When we start paying attention to God's understanding of true love, we learn how the search for love becomes more about defining our expectations and living out a vocation to love one another as He loves us. Before searching for love from another person, we must first be able to find love within ourselves, expressing it in the way we live our lives. Finding true love, most importantly, means finding God—the source of love. Love at first sight happens when we find the benevolent God who searches for a true love through you, with you, in you and for you.

Couples—whether newlyweds or those married for a much longer period of time—sometimes question whether or not they have found that true love in their life. Second guessing is often

 ## TALKING TOGETHER

- Do you believe in love at first sight? Did it happen to you?

- What did you feel when you first laid eyes on each other?

- Did someone introduce you? If so, what was the reason for the introduction? Do you still keep in touch with the person who introduced you? Do you visit the place where you first met?

- What was the most attractive thing about the person you married when you first began dating? Is that still true for you now?

- Was there anything you didn't like as much about the other person? Is that still true for you now?

- What role do you think God played in bringing you together?

- When you first met, did you try to do something different to impress the other person?

- Do your family, friends, or children know what brought the two of you together? Is this a story you're willing to share? Why or why not?

motivated by things like an argument or a lack of romance, leading couples to wonder or daydream about other possibilities.

This can happen at any stage of marriage, but in this chapter, husbands and wives will have an opportunity to strengthen their resolve against such challenges by prayerfully reflecting on their spouse as the "love of their life" and the person that God has specifically chosen for them as His great gift.

Consider your spouse or your future spouse, for a moment. When you first met, were you looking for or really expecting to find Mr. Right? When introduced, did you immediately see the most beautiful girl in the world—the one whom you would carry across the threshold? If you answered "yes," congratulations! I hope it lasts.

If not, have faith! You're not alone. Most happily married couples will say that it wasn't fireworks at first sight; rather, most had to look just a little harder for that true and abiding love. That's what dating is for.

Impatience sometimes tempts couples to imagine that true love will be theirs instantaneously, but reality tells us that it takes years and years (and even more years) to nurture a deep and abiding love. Real love between spouses is far less an instant reality than a lifetime commitment.

It's a lifelong process that begins with learning about oneself, in preparation for an encounter with that special someone-to-be. The phrase "To thine own self be true," may not be from Scripture, but it's still sound advice. Falling in love with another person first requires knowing that you have enough love within yourself to share with someone else. Thus, it is in understanding our own feelings that gives us the maturity necessary to put true love into perspective.

A relationship can easily be threatened if a person confuses "romantic infatuation" with "committed love." People who have been married for a long time sometimes experience romantic feelings for someone other than their own spouse. This feeling, however, does not have to lead to a separation, because simply put, love is not an instant feeling!

Whenever I counsel couples that believe they may be "falling out of love" with each other, I challenge them to reconsider their understanding of love by asking them about their understanding of "love at first sight." My experience has been that couples sometimes start to question their marital love when one or the other of the spouses believes they've discovered "love" in someone else.

Typically, what they're feeling is infatuation; but love is not a feeling. Love is a responsible, lifelong decision. It begins with God's love, followed by an appropriate love of oneself that is nurtured and developed, as we practice Jesus' new command to "love one another" as He loves us.

Healing in these situations may be difficult, but it can and does happen. This only becomes possible, however, once the people involved stop thinking of love as a "fairytale" and instead accept the fact that loving relationships

are a "mystery" that require commitment and patience, in order to be understood. The work of rekindling romantic love takes an appreciation for the fact that love is a process that naturally takes time and patience. Understanding the mysterious process of love may not be simple, but it doesn't have to be frustrating either. It doesn't take a genius to have a loving marriage; it just takes the patience of a saint!

Without a perspective rooted in God, human love can grow tired, old, or boring. Ultimately, it is likely to be short-lived. A saint, on the other hand, realizes that he or she must patiently look for God's love in that other person.

"For God so loved the world that he gave his only Son..." (John 3:16)

This Bible passage provides couples with an assurance of God's love and faithfulness in challenging times, helping them to maintain the love they first discovered in one another "back in the day." When we begin to think of love in those bigger terms, not in fleeting feelings, then we at last begin to understand how God sees love—and how we need to try to see love, as well.

If God wasn't on your mind when you first met as a couple, let not your heart be troubled! Can you at least agree, however, that God knew what He was doing when He brought the two of you together in the first place? That question alone can buy a struggling couple some much-needed time before making a hasty decision to abandon their promise to love. Simply making an effort to investigate God's plan can help the spouses to become saints who will practice faithful love, rather than giving into passing feelings.

Eventually, faith in God becomes the most attractive and beautiful thing a person sees in their spouse. Faithfulness is what married couples vow to each other, and when it's lived out well, it is truly inspirational. Take, for example, a Golden Wedding Anniversary—a rare and beautiful moment that happens when couples are willing to persevere in solving the "mystery" of love. While physical appearances may be the first thing that attracted them to one another, Sacred Scripture explains best what truly caught their eye.

"God created man in his image; in the divine image he created him; male and female he created them." (Genesis 1:27)

Now that's beauty! That's love at first sight!

Look at your spouse through the eyes of faith, which means, with a Godly Love. When you can see your spouse through God's eyes, you may see God working in his or her life. That exciting discovery of God's eternal love could bring about a renewed love for the both of you. This may not happen at first sight, but don't worry; you have a lifetime to keep looking.

 PRAYING TOGETHER

Let us pray: Lord, You are eternally wise! You brought us together for a reason—to help us to find Your presence in our lives. Rekindle within us the fire of love for You and for each other. Each day, when we look at one another, help us to see how Your hand brought us together. When we find it difficult to see You in the other, please move our hearts to seek You within ourselves first, preventing us from criticizing one another too quickly, that we may grow in patience, as we learn how to love with Your love. Most loving Father, help us to remember that our purpose in marriage is to help each other, to love each other, and to bring Your loving presence to each other. We ask this in the name of Your Son, Jesus, our Lord. Amen.

 # DINING TOGETHER

Suggested Menu: Rosemary Roasted Chicken glazed with white creamy wine sauce. Asian vegetable rice and asparagus Parmesan. Dessert: Semi-homemade chocolate chip & walnut cookies with vanilla ice cream.

This menu offers simple but savory flavors. The chicken preparation uses a technique that can easily be altered to different herbs and aromatics. The preparation for the rice keeps things extra easy by using only one pot. And, the semi-homemade dessert keeps the cooking process very easy but inventive. This dish elevates a normal chicken and rice dinner to a whole new romantic level! And, the wine that is used in making the sauce for the chicken pairs perfectly for drinking during the meal.

ROSEMARY ROASTED CHICKEN

2	boneless chicken breasts
1 Tbsp	flour for dredging
1 tsp	flour for creating a roux
1-2 tsp	salt & pepper
1 tsp	garlic powder
1 tsp	fresh rosemary, finely minced
2 Tbsp	olive oil
1 Tbsp	butter
¼ cup	white wine (sauvignon blanc recommended)
½ cup	chicken broth
optional	minced scallion or fresh parsley garnish

Tenderize chicken by lightly pounding it. Season both sides of the chicken with salt, pepper, garlic powder, and freshly minced rosemary. Dredge in flour and shake off excess. Heat olive oil in a large frying pan over medium high heat. Sear chicken for 2 minutes each side or until chicken is golden brown. Remove chicken breasts and set aside. Reduce heat to low and add butter until melted. Add 1 teaspoon of flour to pan and whisk together to create a roux. Add white wine and whisk all the drippings from the bottom of the pan until fully incorporated in the white wine. Simmer for 30 seconds to 1 minute to cook off some of the harshness of the alcohol taste. Add chicken broth and whisk together. Return the chicken breast to the pan and cook for another 10 minutes, uncovered. Season with more salt and pepper if desired.

Option: add garnish with minced scallion greens or fresh minced parsley.

ASIAN VEGETABLE RICE

1 cup	long grain rice
4-6 cups	water
1 cup	frozen mixed vegetables
2 Tbsp	soy sauce
½ tsp	salt
½ tsp	pepper
1 Tbsp	butter

Boil water in pot. Add rice and cook for about 15 minutes, or until rice is soft, but not mushy. Cook rice as you would cook pasta. When rice is cooked to desired texture, drain water from the pot leaving about ¼ cup of water in the pot. Return the pot of rice to the oven and continue to cook over low heat. Add butter, frozen vegetables, salt, pepper, and soy sauce to the rice. Mix rice and cook until frozen vegetables are completely warmed. Fluff rice with fork before serving.

ASPARAGUS PARMESAN

8 stalks	asparagus (4 per person)
2 cups	boiling water
½ tsp	salt
½ tsp	pepper
1 tsp	olive oil
1 tsp	butter
1 clove	fresh garlic, minced
4 tsp	freshly grated Parmesan cheese

Boil water in a frying pan large enough for the asparagus. Cut and discard woody part of the asparagus stalks—i. e. , remove the whitish or brownish part of the asparagus. Rinse asparagus and place in the frying pan of boiling water. Cook asparagus for 2–3 minutes or until it turns bright green. Drain water from the pan leaving about 2–4 teaspoons of water in the pan. Return pan to the stove over medium heat. Add olive oil, butter and garlic to pan and sauté until butter is completely melted. Season with salt and pepper. Grate approximately 4 teaspoons of fresh Parmesan cheese to coat the asparagus, allowing cheese to melt making a light sauce.

SEMI HOMEMADE CHOCOLATE AND WALNUT COOKIE SANDWICH

2 scoops	vanilla ice cream
1 pack	Ready-made chocolate chip cookie mix (enough for 4 large cookies)
¼ cup	walnuts, coarsely chopped or crushed

Preheat oven according to cookie mix instructions. Coarsely crush walnuts in a food processor or place in a plastic bag and lightly pound using the flat side of a small frying pan. Add nuts to the store bought cookie dough and mix until nuts are fully incorporated into the cookie dough. Follow cookie dough instructions, make four cookies, roughly the size of a ping-pong ball. Bake cookies according to instructions. Once cooked, remove and let each cookie cool on a baker's rack. To assemble the cookie, scoop vanilla ice cream on "bottom" part of 2 cookies. Top off with other cookie, to make 2 sandwiches. If you have left over crushed walnuts, roll the sides of the ice cream cookie for extra crunch. Return the cookie to the freezer for about 10 minutes to keep the form of the ice cream cookie. Serve with a garnish of a sprig of fresh mint, and a small warm bowl of your favorite chocolate sauce. If you have kids, you may want to make a few extras to "bribe" your kids for a future favor!

Cooking Tip:
The technique to cook the asparagus can be used for other veggies, such as zucchini, broccoli and cauliflower. To add an extra "crunch" combine some seasoned breadcrumbs with the Parmesan cheese.

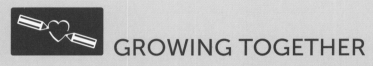

GROWING TOGETHER

Write out a few ideas, thoughts, or prayers on how this chapter can strengthen your marriage.

_____

_____

_____

_____

_____

_____

_____

_____

_____

_____

_____

_____

_____

_____

_____

_____

_____

_____

_____

_____

_____

_____

_____

_____

_____

_____

_____

_____

_____

Chapter 2

Dating Mr. or Ms. Right

*Are You the Perfect Person
For Your Spouse?*

> *A kind mouth multiplies friends, and gracious lips prompt friendly greetings. Let your acquaintances be many, but one in a thousand your confidant... Keep away from your enemies; be on guard with your friends. A faithful friend is a sturdy shelter; he who finds one finds a treasure. A faithful friend is beyond price, no sum can balance his worth. A faithful friend is a life-saving remedy, such as he who fears God finds; for he who fears God behaves accordingly, and his friend will be like himself.*
>
> SIRACH 6:5–6, 13–17

Some people would never even consider seeking relationship advice from a parish priest, but it's not uncommon for married couples—even those who have been together for a long time—to do just that. Often, it's because they're seeking insight into how God might help them come to terms with their difficulties, providing the direction and the guidance they need to navigate through the challenges that are part of every relationship. Sometimes it's simply a matter of seeking ways to improve communication between one another.

It's not just married couples that come to me in search of priestly counsel; those who are dating do as well. For instance, young people in the Confessional sometimes ask for my advice about their girlfriend or boyfriend, engaged couples frequently come in search of guidance in preparation for marriage, and so on.

Sometimes I'm approached for support only after a relationship has ended. After Mass, parents occasionally ask me to pray for a child who is struggling after leaving a long-term relationship. Unfortunately, I've also been called to make hospital and even funeral home visits, when the heartache of a failed relationship has led to self-destructive behavior, sometimes with devastating consequences.

Dating is serious business! This is where the groundwork for marriage begins, and so in this chapter we're going to turn the clock back, so to speak, to examine what our grandparents used to call "courtship."

Whether you've been married for one year or for several decades, a discussion about dating will almost certainly bring back some happy memories. It may even help your relationship in the here and now.

Dating has changed much since I was young. Perhaps the same is true for you as well. I can recall as a young teenager how "third base" meant a peck on a cheek; a "home run" was a wet smack on the lips, and a "grand slam" was a real kiss. In our fast-paced society, however, young people grow up far more quickly than we care to admit; i.e., the bases have changed. First base is an immediate double, and a romantic home run has turned into a full body contact sport—if you know what I mean! This desire to "score" as many runs as quickly as possible can affect the relationship significantly.

In providing counseling, I've noticed that a couple's interactions while dating can have a profound impact on their marriage going forward. If dating was done poorly, e.g., hastily, immaturely, motivated primarily by physical desire, lacking in faithfulness, etc., the couple may suffer from unresolved personal conflicts that make the marital relationship even more challenging than it might otherwise be. Fortunately, however, the opposite is also true.

While many people think that the purpose of dating is to get to know the other person, it may be more accurate to say that it's primarily about gaining self-knowledge. Now this is in no way meant to imply that dating is a self-serving enterprise; rather, it's simply to say that dating should help us learn a great deal about ourselves, what we can offer the other person, and what kind of person we want to be for the one we love.

Those who fail to approach dating as an opportunity to develop a healthy degree of self-knowledge are typically unaware of the quirky behaviors they bring to the relationship. (And believe me, we all have them!) Frequently, such people tend to be selfish. They often seek partners in life who can fill their need for a "savior" to deliver them from themselves. Usually, people who fit this description are incapable of the self-giving that is necessary for a healthy relationship.

Dating done well, however, can help us to develop the self-awareness that leads to the confidence we need to stand firm in our convictions, to be reliable and steady and true. Ultimately, this brings the couple closer to God, His laws and His love. It helps the individuals involved live out the challenge set forth in the Scripture passage at the beginning of this chapter, reminding them that they must be "faithful friends," both with God and with one another.

 TALKING TOGETHER

- What are your thoughts about dating services? Arranged Marriages? Family members that try to set up dates for each other?

- What are some of the differences you see in the way people date today, compared to before you were married? Are we better off now? Have we lost the idea of "courtship" in dating?

- What are (what would be, what were) some of your fears for your children as they begin the dating process?

- Would your spouse be the person your parents would pick for you?

- Would you be the person your spouse's parents would pick for their child?

- While you were dating, what did you learn about yourself? How did your dating experience help you make the decision that your spouse is Mr./Ms. Right?

- What were some of your best dates? What were some of your worse dates? Were there times when dating went too far? What can we teach young people about dating boundaries?

- Is there something you always wanted to ask your spouse while you were dating but were too afraid to ask?

This approach to dating helps us to remain aware that we alone cannot carry life's burdens for our significant other; rather, the person who truly wishes to serve as a "sturdy shelter" for their beloved is the one who will point to the real Savior, Jesus Christ, the One who carries all of our burdens with us and for us, in the form of the Cross.

With so much at stake, it's beneficial for couples at all stages of marriage to occasionally make time to prayerfully consider their dating experience. Doing so can sometimes shed light on any lingering issues that may be contributing to the challenges they're currently facing.

Reflecting on those distant days of courtship can even be of benefit to the next generation. For example, it can better equip parents whose children are dating or are about to begin dating. Grandparents can become even better listeners and advice-givers for those grandchildren who would prefer not to talk to mom or dad about a special friend.

At the very least, a reflective walk down lovers' lane can put a smile on a couple's face by rekindling happy memories. So go ahead and talk with one another about what life was like when you were dating. The more you talk about it, the more you can learn from this important relationship-building experience.

Whatever you do, though, don't just talk about it! With so many lasting gifts made available through a good dating experience, there's no reason it should cease simply because you're married. There's still a lot to learn about yourself and your spouse, and going on dates can go a long way toward strengthening your marriage.

Continuing the dating experience can also make couples better guides for others seeking relationship advice—like children or single friends. Even if kids don't ask particular

questions about dating, the witness given by parents who strengthen their marriage through regular dates provides children with a positive testimony of parental love. It edifies them and gives witness to the importance of spending quality time with people we love. Parents who demonstrate an appropriate level of personal affection for one another teach their children valuable lessons about intimacy by example.

In a parish where I previously served, one of the priests organized a special event for married parishioners called "Couples Date Night." It was a huge success! The couples would chip in to pay for a few trusted babysitters to watch over the children, so the couples could reserve an entire evening for themselves. Through the generosity and support of donors, couples would then dine on a romantic dinner, listen to a speaker who offered insights about marriage, and then discuss ways to strengthen their love for God and for one another. The couples were able to share a long overdue, theologically motivated, romantic date. They had fun with a purpose! Doing this as a parish-based program let all of the couples know that they're not the only married people who could use a little help staying focused and in love.

As a parish priest, I've met far too many couples that have lost that "spark" in their marriage. Something as simple as going out on a real date, however, can kick-start a relationship's creative nature. An example of a good date is one in which each person tries to do something special for the other, and even a small act of this kind can really strengthen a couple's sense of togetherness.

For those married couples who do venture to go on a date, they often limit themselves to just a movie or something similarly predictable. My suggestion is to do something fun, a little more interactive, and not so passive. Do something that will bring out that sense of adventure, joy, and excitement that is still in you! It doesn't have to be expensive. A good date for married people can be any activity that breaks up the routine—something to remind the couple of life's excitement—similar to the way things were when they first started dating!

When a married couple takes the time to learn more about themselves and one another through a date, they naturally tend to reflect on the steps they took before making the deeper commitment to one another in marriage. Just talking about how one date after another eventually led to your wedding day—now that would be a great dinner date conversation!

Dinner dates for married couples work. At a Grace Before Meals-sponsored event, a group of married couples won the auction prize—a personally prepared dinner by me. During the meal and in between courses, I peppered the conversation with questions, many of which made the couples pause, think, share, giggle, and sometimes even blush like young lovers. They were surprised to find out how much they learned about each other from only one flavor-filled dinner seasoned with just a few intentional questions.

The most common excuse married couples seem to make for not going on a date is busyness.

"I don't have time for that! After all, we're married—we already know each other!"

If you find yourself "too busy" for your spouse, then you just might be lacking some of the self-knowledge that is required to be a good spouse in the first place. If left unaddressed, that attitude can quickly lead to the downhill slide toward ambivalence, loneliness, and ultimately a breakup.

Fortunately, the excuse of "busyness" has a simple remedy: reality. When you were first dating, long before marriage even entered into the conversation, you may have been just as busy as you are today, but you and your spouse-to-be enjoyed one another's company so much that you just made the time. Ask yourself, was your busy schedule more important than spending quality time with the person you were falling in love with then? No! Admit it; nothing was more important than keeping that relationship alive and well. So why should anything change now?

Now don't get me wrong; dating is work, but it's also an investment in your future together. Like any other investment, you need to continue making contributions to that "account" throughout your relationship. That's why keeping a balanced schedule is critical; it allows couples to devote time to the important things and the important people in their lives, like the occasional date with their spouse.

Now that you're convinced, I need to tell you that when married couples go on a date, the intention is a little different than it is for single people. Married couples are no longer wondering, "Is this person right for me?" That question was definitively answered with the words, "I do!"

A date between married persons inspires other, equally important questions, e.g., "Do I always put my husband first in my life?" "What kind of man do I want to be for my wife?" "What do I need to change about myself to be a more loving and more lovable person for my spouse?" "How will we teach our children about loving relationships?" Questions such as these, as well as those in the Talking Together section, can spur meaningful conversation for any married couple on a date.

Ultimately, each date night will help rekindle the love that you and your spouse felt when you were dating as singles. Be encouraged to find out why God—the ultimate matchmaker—brought the two of you together in the first place. If it's not apparent already, you may come to realize that the purpose of your attraction was not based simply on romantic feelings, economic status, family pressure, or cultural traditions. Your dates—the ones that led to your marriage—were an important part of God's loving plan to bless you with a hope-filled life this side of Heaven.

Just as Eve complemented Adam, your spouse fulfills the deepest longing in you: to love another as God loves you. You can demonstrate that on your next date, and you don't even need your parents' blessing; you already have God's!

 # PRAYING TOGETHER

Let us pray: Father of Love, You knew what we were looking for, when we were dating one another. You know that loving one another as a couple will require an appropriate amount of self-love as well as love of You. When we were dating, we may have done things that didn't help our marriage. Please forgive us for any impatience, lack of faithfulness, lack of chastity, or sincere honesty. Now that we are married, help us to see how much we need to continue getting to know one another in the ways you intend. Life is mysterious, and our relationship could always use a little more freshness. We know that You can give us this renewal if only we are willing to approach each day with an eager attentiveness and a desire to better love one another. While dating as a married couple may seem strange to us, please give us the courage to do the things that will strengthen our relationship, including a romantic night just for the "Three" of us—me, my spouse, and You, the Lord of Love. Amen.

 **DINING TOGETHER**

Suggested Menu: Bacon and Butternut Squash Brandy Creamy Penne Pasta. Pan-Sautéed Broccoli, as a warm salad or side dish. Dessert: Fresh Fruit Macedonia in a Sambuca liqueur. Sambuca is an intense anise-flavored Italian after-dinner drink. This dessert offers a refreshing flavor that cuts through the creamy pasta you just shared.

Savory and sweet makes for a perfect flavor profile for creamy pasta sauces. The brandy-infused dish gives the cream sauce a rich and elegant flavor that couples can interchange with other sweet liqueurs, such as cognac or sherry. Vegetables, like broccoli, don't have to be boring! This simple but tasty pan preparation for the broccoli retains the crunch and freshness, highlighting the subtle flavors with a light butter sauté and seasoned breadcrumbs. You can serve the broccoli as a side dish or as a warmed salad after the pasta—like many Europeans would do. For dessert, enjoy something fresh, with a burst of anise-flavored glaze over your favorite fresh fruits.

BACON AND BUTTERNUT SQUASH BRANDY CREAMY PENNE PASTA

½ lb	penne pasta, cooked *al dente*
4 strips	thick-cut bacon, cut into thin strips
1 cup	butternut squash, diced into ⅛" cubes
1 small	white onion, diced
1 clove	garlic, finely minced
1 cup	brandy
1 Tbsp	butter
2 tsp	all-purpose flour
1 cup	chicken stock
2 tsp	Parmesan cheese, shaved or grated
2 Tbsp	fresh parsley, finely minced

Boil pasta per instructions. When pasta is cooked *al dente* (translated: "to the tooth," describing the preferred texture of pasta, which is not mushy and is slightly chewy), drain water completely, then add a light drizzle of olive oil. Toss pasta together, and set aside. Cook bacon in a large sauté pan over medium-high heat, until fatty parts of the bacon become crispy. Remove bacon and drain oil, leaving about 2 teaspoons of bacon grease in the pan. In the same pan, sauté the butternut squash, onions, and garlic, until squash becomes soft and onions become translucent, about 2–3 minutes. Add brandy and either flambé or cook away from an exposed flame for 2–3 minutes. Add butter and flour, and mix together, until sauce thickens. Add chicken stock, and stir together. Return the bacon and pasta to the pan, and cook until sauce thickens. Sprinkle Parmesan cheese and fresh minced parsley to finish the dish.

PAN SAUTÉ BROCCOLI

8 florets	broccoli (4 per person)
½ cup	water
1 tsp	butter
¼ tsp	salt
¼ tsp	pepper
¼ tsp	red pepper flakes
¼ tsp	garlic powder
1 Tbsp	Italian seasoned breadcrumbs

Boil water in a frying pan over high heat. Add the broccoli, and occasionally turn the broccoli over, so that all sides turn a bright green. When the broccoli turns bright green, and water is almost evaporated, add butter, salt, pepper, red pepper flakes, and garlic powder, and sauté for 1–2 minutes. Remove from heat, and sprinkle Italian seasoned breadcrumbs over all sides of the broccoli. Serve immediately.

SAMBUCA FRUIT MACEDONIA

1	apple, diced into small ¼" pieces or sections
1	orange, peeled and sectioned
1	banana, cut and cubed into ¼" pieces
½ cup	grapes (white or red), washed and cut in half
2 tsp	granulated sugar
½	lemon, juiced
2 Tbsp	Sambuca liqueur
optional	fresh mint, for garnish

Add all chopped fruit and sugar to a bowl, and mix with lemon juice. Drizzle the Sambuca liqueur, and gently mix together, or allow the liqueur to marinate the decorated fruit plate. Place fruit in the refrigerator to marinate and chill. Decorate a plate with the fruit in any artistic fashion. A simple and elegant presentation would be to scoop the fruit in a martini glass with a fresh sprig of mint.

Cooking Tip:
Instead of eating a cold salad with a warm pasta dish, try a warm side dish with the pasta. You may wind up liking it so much that you'll combine these two dishes for less of a mess and a unique flavor in every bite! You can even create your very own specialty pasta sauce with this technique.

GROWING TOGETHER

Write out a few thoughts, ideas, prayers, or even memories about your dates and your desire to continue dating and getting to know your spouse.

_____
_____
_____
_____
_____
_____
_____
_____
_____
_____
_____
_____
_____
_____
_____
_____
_____
_____
_____
_____
_____
_____
_____
_____

Chapter 3

On Bended Knee

The Proposal of a Lifetime

> *In the sixth month, the angel Gabriel was sent from God to a town of Galilee called Nazareth, to a virgin betrothed to a man named Joseph of the house of David... And coming to her, he said, 'Hail, favored one! The Lord is with you.' But she was greatly troubled at what was said and pondered what sort of greeting this might be... Mary said, 'Behold I am the handmaid of the Lord. May it be done to me according to your word!'*

LUKE 1:26–30, 38

Hearing engaged couples recount the details of their marriage proposal amuses, fascinates, and oftentimes inspires me. In fact, I begin my first pre-marriage meeting with the question, "How did you propose?"

You may think it's just an icebreaker or a conversation starter, but I have pastoral reasons for asking. The way the marriage proposal happens can say a great deal about the maturity level of the couple, providing several key bits of information that help me determine which direction the couple is likely to take in marriage.

If the couple wants their marriage to be blessed by God, it begins with a proposal blessed by God. The Scripture passage at the beginning of the chapter represents just that type of proposal. The Archangel Gabriel, speaking with God's authority, invites Mary into a deep, spousal union with God. Not coincidentally, paintings of The Annunciation often depict the Angel on bended knee, imagery we often associate with a marriage proposal. Though surprised, Mary trusted God enough to say "yes" to His Will, and that's what couples do (or ought to do) in every marriage proposal, respond with a "yes" to God's Will, whatever it may be.

The proposal represents a uniquely significant moment in a relationship. While it is entirely likely that the couple has already discussed their desire to get married many times prior, officially "popping the question" firmly establishes sincerity. It's a big moment!

I often remind couples, however, that even though their engagement is a sure sign of their growing closeness, this pales in comparison to the spiritual, and even the physical, closeness they will experience once joined in Sacramental Marriage. Just the same, engagement is a truly crucial step, propelling the couple into the final stages of preparation for the blessed event. In culinary terms, the food is being plated. Soon it will be time for the dish to be served and consumed.

Blessed Pope John Paul II identified and described three preparatory stages leading to marriage: remote, proximate, and immediate.

The remote stage encompasses the experiences of the individuals growing up, prior to the dating stage. It includes their experience of the relationships in their childhood home, what they experienced from their parents' marriage, and how society, media, and pop culture portrayed marriage in those formative years. In sum, these experiences have a considerable effect on the way an individual views marriage. In fact, by the time most couples approach the Church to go through marriage classes, a great deal of preparation and subconscious formation has already occurred, whether they realize it or not.

Unfortunately, the number of children growing up in broken families continues to rise. The experience of living through his/her parents' separation greatly affects an individual's view on marriage. Young and impressionable minds are bombarded with television programs depicting dramatic courtroom divorces and desperate, unfaithful housewives. In a climate such as this, how can a person be expected to enter the next stage of marriage preparation—the proximate stage—without having been negatively affected?

The proximate stage involves serious or exclusive dating. In this phase, a couple moves from a more casual relationship to a deeper level of commitment, sometimes with an unspoken understanding that they are moving toward marriage. This is a time for couples to seriously discern a possible future together by considering how their current activities, modes of communication, and expressions of faith will affect their marriage. It may be good for a couple in the proximate stage to seek the advice of a "mentor" couple or couples. Observing and learning from married couples that demonstrate a faithful and committed love—such as parents/future in-laws, a boss and his wife, or other couples from church—can be a very useful exercise.

During the proximate stage, it's especially important for a couple to draw closer to God, specifically, so they can learn how to pray together as a couple. In so doing, they invite God to enter more deeply into their love, becoming a part of their relationship and helping them to discern their future together. After all, He's the One who brings engaged and married couples together in the first place! At least, we hope.

Once the couple begins to recognize that their meeting was not just chance but God's providence, then the next important step occurs—the proposal!

 ## TALKING TOGETHER

- How did your proposal happen? Did it go off as you planned? What were the words used and the response given?

- Who were the first people who knew of your intentions to marry? And why did you tell them about your plans?

- What were you thinking while selecting the ring? What does your wedding ring mean to you now?

- If you've been married for a number of years, is the excitement you had on that day something you are able to recall? If not, why?

- Do you ever celebrate the proposal day as an anniversary to remember?

- If your proposal took place over a meal, do you remember what you ate or the name of the restaurant where it occurred?

- Have your children ever heard of how mommy or daddy proposed? Will you ever tell them?

- What are your thoughts about requesting permission for a daughter's hand in marriage?

This brings the couple to the immediate stage—the final stage of preparation for Sacramental Marriage, one that will change their lives forever. The immediacy of the wedding day becomes quite palpable. Depending on how the parents feel about their future son or daughter in-law, there could be an immediate sense of excitement and joy—or tremendous fear, hesitancy, and disappointment.

But before all that happens, someone has to officially propose!

Having heard more proposal stories than I can count, it seems that all of them share a common characteristic: things never go quite as perfectly as intended.

Whenever I ask a couple, "How did the proposal happen?" I usually get an embarrassed laugh, followed by a sweet sigh of happy memories. I pray that the joy of that moment lives on in the hearts and minds of all couples—no matter how long they've been married.

Besides providing a glimpse of the personality of this future couple, the proposal establishes important facts for the couple to consider before they spend the rest of their lives together. They must immediately begin to decide how to make this natural human love more like the supernatural Love of God.

For most couples, the proposal requires following up with very practical things: telling their families, determining a wedding date, booking the hall, shopping for the wedding dress, picking colors for bridesmaids' dresses, and conducting food tasting for the reception—always a plus for faithful foodies. As good and as fun as that may be, I warn couples to, most importantly, make sure the wedding day reflects God's Love working in their lives. Their marriage plans ought to resemble a Sacrament and not a coronation. I advise couples to consult God as the ultimate wedding coordinator. Newly engaged couples are oftentimes in such a rush after the proposal that I try to slow them down. I remind them of the more realistic aspects of married life and how to use this precious time to learn how best to love one another.

Remember, if the proposal puts the couple on a trajectory towards marriage, then ultimately, that proposal should put the couple on the trajectory to Heaven. Just think about what is said (or should be said) in a good marriage proposal. Reflect once again on God's proposal to Mary, and you'll see how God was inviting her to celebrate the wedding banquet in Heaven.

First, a good proposal shouldn't be a complete surprise.

In Mary's case, while she was surprised, she was certainly prepared to listen to God. Again, paintings of The Annunciation oftentimes show Mary in a posture of prayer. In other words, the angel found her already listening to God. In prayer, God does talk with us—that's the purpose of prayer. In good proposals, the proposer determines that they have dated well enough (notice, I didn't say "long enough") to know God is drawing them closer to a sacred love.

In most traditional proposals, the groom would even ask the father for the daughter's hand in marriage. Again, that shouldn't surprise anyone. Even though family members may not exactly know when, they are hopefully smart enough to know that it will eventually happen. Even though asking the father for his daughter's hand in marriage is not canonically expected, I find this gesture encouraging, because it establishes an important fact: the groom respects the bride's family and sees how good communication with his in-laws will be essential to making this relationship work. It may also be a good idea to ask God the Father what He thinks about the marriage, as well. In other words, before the proposal, there needs to be even more prayer! That way, even if the bride's father may not completely approve, at least the groom can have the blessing of Our Father in Heaven.

Another aspect of the proposal is the search for the ring. In marriage, the mission is to live the significance of the ring—an unbroken union. The ring represents the personal sacrifice grooms traditionally undergo in order to afford just the right symbol that will grace the hand of the person he holds in marriage. Every couple I know takes that part of the marriage proposal very seriously. And if they remember to also pray about what that ring symbolizes, then the marriage proposal will be blessed with more than just the bride's "yes"; it will be blessed with God's insight.

I joke with couples on the wedding day by saying there are three rings in marriage: the engagement ring, the wedding ring, and the suffer-ring! Okay, I know that's corny, but the point is that getting the perfect ring isn't a matter of cost—it's a matter of sacrifice. And sacrifice will be required if the meaning of the ring—an unbroken union—is to be both a hallmark of your wedding day and truly realized in your marriage.

Another part of the proposal is the flexibility required in planning for it. I've never heard of a wedding proposal that went off perfectly. The forecast didn't call for rain. Someone else reserved the table you wanted. Unexpected intruders cramped your privacy. Or your then boyfriend simply got so nervous that his "Will you marry me?" became an incoherent babble. But the fact that someone tried to plan a perfect day is a good thing, and it tells a lot about the seriousness of this invitation to marriage. But planning should not be limited to a proposal lasting only a few seconds. The wording of the proposal should reflect a couple's interior desire and, indeed, the proposer's approach to prayer. After all, the one who proposes is actually praying that the other person says "yes!"

Why should an already married couple reconsider the original proposal? First, it's fun. Second, it will show how the couple has grown in their understanding of marriage. Third, it will reveal the deeper meaning of their love.

If the proposal you gave was truly from God, then the bended knee will be met with a response similar to Mary's response to God, "May it be done to me according to your word!" For modern couples, that phrase has been translated to that simple word, "yes," followed up with tears, hugs, kisses, and a perhaps even a sigh of relief. After all, doing God's Will is the only option for marital happiness.

 PRAYING TOGETHER

Let us pray: Loving God, You allowed us to experience the same joy, anticipation, and sense of responsibility the Blessed Virgin Mary felt when You came to her through the message of an Archangel. Help us to see that marriage is not a "right," but a "gift" that You give to us, in order to give to each other. Lord, help us to remember the great sense of responsibility on the day of our engagement. Help us never to forget the tremendous feeling of love and joy from that day, especially on days when we may be tempted to reconsider why we both agreed to marriage. When the engagement was officially announced, we probably didn't have the best understanding of what would be required of marriage, and perhaps we still don't. God, help us to look back on that important moment of our lives—the proposal—and help us to see how You have been trying to guide us every step of the way. For the times when we put You on the backburner, help us to seek forgiveness. And, like Mary, help us to be docile to what You have planned for us, knowing that we were not only saying "yes" to our spouse, but also to You! With Mary's prayers, we ask this through Christ our Lord. Amen.

 ## DINING TOGETHER

Suggested Menu: Pan-Roasted Teriyaki Steak and Veggie Skewers, served with a warm Pan-Roasted Red Potato Salad. Dessert: Strawberry Crepes with whipped cream.

Shish kebabs can make for an easy and delicious meal. With a few unique ingredients, this once common street food becomes a gourmet experience that helps couples explore different flavors of different countries. It's almost a complete meal on a stick! The roasted potato salad adds the creaminess and warmth to balance the savory flavors of the skewers. For dessert, travel to France with an easy crepe mixture that can be stored and used later for other meal preparations other than desserts.

CUBED TERIYAKI STEAK AND VEGGIE SKEWERS

½ cup	soy sauce
½ cup	brown sugar
½	lemon, juiced
2 Tbsp	rice wine or white wine vinegar
1	shallot, finely minced
1 clove	garlic, finely minced
1 tsp	sesame seed oil, for marinade
1 tsp	salt
2 tsp	hot sauce (your favorite brand)
6-8 oz	New York strip steak, cut 1" cubes to create 8-10 equally-sized pieces (fat trimmed)
8-10	cherry tomatoes
½ med.	red onion, cut approximately ¼" to create 8-10 pieces
2 tsp	sesame seed oil, for cooking the skewers
	4 wooden or metal skewers 6-8" in length

Prepare marinade for the skewers by combining soy sauce, brown sugar, lemon juice, rice wine (or white wine) vinegar, minced shallot, minced garlic, 1 teaspoon of sesame seed oil, salt, and hot sauce. Stir until ingredients are fully incorporated or until brown sugar is completely dissolved. Assemble the four skewers by placing an interchanging of beef, tomato, and onion combination. You should have enough pieces to make four skewers, with equal pieces of meat, onion, and tomato on each skewer. Pack these ingredients tightly together to allow for an even cooking process. Place skewers in a nonreactive container, and pour the marinade over the skewers. Refrigerate for at least one hour, maximum four hours. When ready to cook, brush sesame seed oil on a grill pan or flat skillet over medium-high heat. Make sure the skewers fit evenly onto the grill pan. If necessary, use smaller skewers. Cook the skewers for 3–5 minutes on each side, or until veggies begin to caramelize. When cooked, remove skewers from the grill pan, and let them rest a few minutes before serving.

PAN ROASTED RED POTATO SALAD

2-3 med	red potatoes, cut into ½" chunks
2-3 cups	water
2 tsp	olive oil
1 clove	garlic, minced
½	red onion, cut into thin strips
1	celery stalk, minced into roughly ⅛" pieces
2 Tbsp	mayonnaise
2 tsp	lemon juice
1 tsp	salt
1 tsp	pepper
1 tsp	paprika
1 tsp	fresh parsley, minced (substitute: ½ tsp dried parsley flakes)

Add potatoes to a large skillet of water. Boil water, and cook potatoes until fork tender, approximately 6–8 minutes from the time the water starts to boil. Drain water completely. Add olive oil, garlic, onions, and celery to potatoes, and sauté for 2–4 minutes, allowing some caramelizing to occur on the vegetables. In a large mixing bowl, combine mayonnaise, lemon juice, salt, pepper, paprika, and fresh parsley. Add the potatoes, and gently stir together. Can be served warm or refrigerated to serve chilled.

Option: For a smoky-flavored potato salad, grill the potatoes on a lightly greased grill pan over medium heat, and cook until fork tender. Once cooked, combine all of the other ingredients, as instructed.

STRAWBERRY CREPES)

1 cup	all-purpose flour
½ tsp	salt
1	egg
1	egg yolk
1 ½ cups	milk, divided
2 Tbsp	melted butter
1-2 tsp	confectioners' sugar

Crepe batter: Mix flour and salt in a bowl. Add egg, egg yolk, and half of milk and whisk together. Add melted butter and the rest of the milk, until the batter is light and smooth. Let the batter sit at room temperature for about half hour before using. Do not refrigerate. This recipe will make more crepes than you need for a dessert shared by two people (makes 10–15 crepes depending on thickness of each crepe). This batter will keep in the refrigerator for a few days, if placed in a sealed container. If using refrigerated crepe mix, allow the batter to get to room temperature before use.

To cook the crepes: Heat a large nonstick frying pan or flat skillet over medium heat. Apply nonstick spray. Use about ⅛ cup of batter, and pour slowly into the center of the pan, tilting the pan from side-to-side in a circular fashion, until the majority of the flat surface of the pan is covered with the batter. Cook batter for about 1–2 minutes or until the bottom of crepe turns golden brown. Use a long spatula to gently flip the crepes. Add 2 heaping tablespoons of the strawberry filling to center of the crepe, spreading over a 1 inch thick strip from the top to bottom of the crepe (see following recipe). Flip the sides of the crepe to the center, completely covering the strawberry filling. Remove from the pan, and place crepe on a plate. Sift confectioner's sugar over the crepe, and serve with a dollop of whipped cream and a garnish of a fresh sprig of mint. Drizzle the chocolate berry-infused sauce over crepes. (see following recipe)

STRAWBERRY FILLING

1 Tbsp	butter
1 Tbsp	fresh lemon juice
2 Tbsp	granulated sugar
2 cups	fresh strawberries, washed, stems removed, and sliced thinly
optional	Confectioner's or powdered sugar (with a sifter)
optional	whipped cream
optional	fresh sprig of mint
optional	1–2 Tbsp of chocolate chips (white, dark, semi-sweet)

Prepare strawberry filling by melting butter in a small saucepan. Add lemon juice and granulated sugar, until sugar is completely dissolved. Add the strawberries, and sauté for 1–2 minutes. Remove from heat, and set aside. If the berries release their juices, drain into a small bowl, and use only the solid pieces to fill the crepes.

Option: Add 1–2 Tbsp chocolate chip pieces to the berry juice, and melt together to make a chocolate strawberry-infused sauce to drizzle over each crepe.

Cooking Tip:
You can fill the crepe with just about anything you want, from chocolate chips, to any fruit, even vegetables, savory meats, and spicy marinara sauce with melted cheese. Crepes are not just for dessert, so use the leftover crepe batter to make breakfast or a simple lunch or dinner the next day!

Grace Before Meals | Spicing Up Married Life

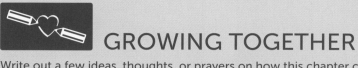

GROWING TOGETHER

Write out a few ideas, thoughts, or prayers on how this chapter can strengthen your marriage.

_____

_____

_____

_____

_____

_____

_____

_____

_____

_____

_____

_____

_____

_____

_____

_____

_____

_____

_____

_____

_____

_____

_____

_____

_____

_____

_____

Chapter 4

The Wedding Day

A Blessing or a Blur

> [Jesus] said in reply,
>
> Have you not read that from the beginning the Creator 'made them male and female' and said, 'For this reason a man shall leave his father and mother and be joined to his wife, and the two shall become one flesh?' So they are no longer two, but one flesh. Therefore, what God has joined together, no human being must separate.

MATTHEW 19:4–6

The wedding day should be one of the most beautiful, prayerful, and memorable days in a couple's life. So why do so many people say that for them—no matter how special— their wedding day was just a blur?

If you're preparing to be married, this chapter can help make this day one of the most blessed days of your married life and, hopefully, help you to remember all the wonderful details. No matter what, this day will change your life forever; you won't want to forget it! If you've been married a while, this chapter will give you a Godly perspective of your wedding day and help you to see the blessings in the blur.

After conducting counseling sessions with couples struggling in their marriage, I am convinced that reflecting on the details of the wedding day is helpful for putting marital problems in perspective. Calling to mind the songs, the specific prayers, and the sacred gestures of the ceremony can help couples get through the rough patches. It helps them to reestablish their roots in the reality of their promise, and it humbles them to remember that it is vows, not problems, that last forever.

When couples first come to me to discuss marriage preparation, it's not uncommon for their focus to be very different than my own. Oftentimes couples want to talk about flowers, the length of the aisle runners, the number of

attendants, the music selections, etc., i.e., all the frills of the ceremony. I sometimes surprise them by saying, "I will talk about your wedding day plans only when I can be assured that you are first trying to focus on a lifetime of marriage and not just the wedding day."

Whether a couple knows it or not, being the official witness for a couple's wedding ceremony is tough work. It's so challenging that some priests have been known to say they'd rather do ten funerals than one wedding! Why? Well, managing a couple's expectations (and sometimes their demands) can sometimes be very challenging.

For many couples, especially those who are overly influenced by the ceremonies they've seen in movies or on television, the wedding day has been downgraded from a solemn act of Holy Communion in a house of prayer to something more akin to a Hollywood spectacle. The drama factor can reduce the sacred moment to a three-ring circus, sometimes to the point of making a priest wonder if he's playing a role on a new primetime reality show called "The Wedding Day!"

The Church, on the other hand, believes that a spiritual depth should permeate the wedding ceremony, setting a couple not just on the path to married life, but on the way to eternal life. That's the kind of focus all couples occasionally need to regain!

When God is the focus and foundation for a marriage, even the biggest wedding day mishaps can't interfere with the essence of this grace-filled event. Unfortunately, sometimes even the most well-rehearsed, minutely detailed wedding plans can go wrong, and the ceremony can easily become a comedy of errors (or, in the case of the couple, a tragedy!)

Over the years, I, along with my brother priests and other wedding ministers, have seen wedding dress malfunctions, flower girl trip-ups, and ring bearers engaging in pillow fights—with the rings still attached! I've endured poorly selected music and even worse singing. I've seen grooms passing out and actually had an altar server vomit! I even had to break up an argument between in-laws the day before a wedding.

One of my all-time "favorite" botched wedding moments involves a couple who, instead of simply recessing to applause, wanted the more dramatic gesture of releasing butterflies.

 TALKING TOGETHER

- What do you remember most about your wedding day? Do remember what you thought was the most important thing about that day? Do you still think that was the most important thing?

- Have you recently looked at your wedding pictures? Have you changed that much? If so, how?

- If you were to plan your wedding all over again, knowing what you know now, what would it look like?

- Can you remember the people who served as your bridesmaids and groomsmen? What are they doing now? Have they been a part of your marriage and not just a part of your wedding day? How?

- Have you kept in touch with the minister who witnessed your ceremony? Did he give you any advice that you still remember (and follow) today? Did he give you any advice that you did not follow? Why not? Do you wish you had?

- Which parts of the actual ceremony did you appreciate the most? Have you ever repeated your vows to each other since that day?

- What advice would you give to couples now preparing for their own wedding? Is there anything you could say to help them save money? Was there a particular Scripture reading that you would recommend they consider using for their wedding ceremony?

- Can you tell if you've grown spiritually since the day of your wedding? If not, how can you and your spouse focus on growing together spiritually, as a couple?

For the couple, this was a big deal. Well, even though I advised them to consider keeping things simpler, if for no other reason than the logistical challenges associated with a butterfly release in a small church, the couple was adamant that it would help them remember their day forever. (Funny, I thought the beautiful prayers and vows would be what they would remember!)

On top of that, this plan came with a big price tag; that box of winged insects cost more than the church donation!

When the time came to show their love to the world, the bride and groom thrust the opened box toward Heaven, only to have one or two butterflies come fluttering out while the rest, suspended somewhere between dead and dying, fell to the ground. It was an unforgettable moment alright, watching the best-laid plans wriggling to death right there on the church stairs.

Morbid? Perhaps, but this is a good illustration of how any attempt to make something other than faith the highlight of the wedding day—no matter how pretty the idea may seem—can overshadow its true meaning.

It's a time to pray, not to play, a day for sacred celebration, not spectacle!

By now you must be thinking that I somehow take pleasure in seeing dramatic plans going awry, but I most definitely do not! In fact, I do my very best to make sure that the wedding day is the most sacred, prayerful, beautiful, and therefore the most joyful moment in the couple's life. As a priest, I truly want the wedding day to be as memorable for the bride and the groom as my ordination is for me—the day that I stood at the altar to give myself to my bride, the Church. At that sacred moment, I guarantee there were no butterflies—not even in my stomach.

To prepare couples for marriage, I try to give them not only care and attention, but also some challenging exercises that will transform them into witnesses of love. Inviting God into the marriage is the most important thing a couple can do to make their wedding something beautiful to behold! You see, it is their love for God and one another that will make the ceremony a grand reflection of what marriage truly is—not the frills!

Couples who take the spiritual side of marriage seriously oftentimes have less expensive and more beautiful ceremonies than their counterparts. I've seen congregations in joy-inspired tears as a couple recites their vows. I've witnessed family members and friends looking on in awe as a couple dedicates flowers that symbolically seek prayers of intercession from Heaven. I've heard of broken families reconciling during the sign of peace, and I've even had guests tell me after the ceremony that their own marital difficulties were somehow healed by the prayers and the witness of the couple.

"… So we, though many, are one body in Christ and individually parts of one of another" (Romans 12:5)

The unity in the Body of Christ is such that the Sacrament of Marriage has a profound effect on more than just the happy couple. When God is invited to be the centerpiece of a marriage, it becomes an occasion of grace that enriches all marriages, indeed all of society, by revealing the true meaning of love to the world!

Theologically, the Church understands the husband as a sacred sign that points the way to Jesus (the Bridegroom) and the wife as she who signifies the Church (His Bride). Together they make God sacramentally present in their commitment to one another. When the bride and the groom come together at the altar, therefore, the congregation is given a glimpse of the kind of love that God has for us as His beloved. That is why marriage is a sacrament—a visible sign of invisible Grace.

The words "I do" are very similar to the word "amen." These words signify the couple's consent, binding them in a covenant relationship that is founded in God, sealed by Him, and made manifest in their hearts. A lack of prayerful preparation before the wedding day has led far too many couples to say "I do" without fully understanding the meaning of the words. This can reduce their perception of what in God's eyes is the solemn promise of an eternal bond to a tepid "I guess so," or "sure, why not?" We see convincing evidence of this lack of understanding in the growing number of broken marriages.

There is still, however, very good news for your marriage! The fact that you are reading this book is a sure sign that you take your marriage seriously. If you were unable to recognize the spiritual insights presented in this chapter at the time of your wedding, don't despair! Simply treat these reflections as an invitation to renew your intentions before God and each other—this time with neither frills nor fanfare.

Those who have been married for any length of time at all realize that the real cost of nurturing an enduring relationship has nothing to do with the grandeur of the reception, the hassle of hiring a photographer, lining up tuxedo rentals, arranging the flowers or scheduling a limousine. Likewise, it doesn't take a fancy ceremony to renew one's vows. It takes faith!

I encourage all married couples to consider renewing their vows prayerfully, with the Godly focus presented herein. Whether you decide to do it after dinner, once a month, every time you go to church, or once a year on your anniversary, this can be a wonderful way for couples to reacquaint themselves with the true meaning and purpose of marriage.

As you renew your "I do," remember that God keeps His promises to both of you. If you allow God to truly be a part of your marriage, He can bring you the kind of joy that will last a lifetime. God always loves us, even when we act unlovable. He forgives unfaithfulness, because He loves us faithfully. God's presence in a marriage teaches couples how to love each other as He does. Since God is love, how can a couple stay married without Him?

In time, the wedding day for that famous couple in Cana may have become just a blur, even for them, but I'm sure they always remembered the miracle that Jesus performed for them on their special day: changing water into the best of wines. In so doing, the Lord demonstrated that His presence at the ceremony (and even the reception to follow) brings about the greatest of miracles. He can change the celebration into a Sacrament for life.

How much did that miracle cost? Nothing, except for great faith!

 # PRAYING TOGETHER

Let us pray: Father, You made marriage the union between man and woman as a sign of Your covenant with Your Church. Give us the grace to say "yes" to each other and to You! Lord, when we struggle in our marriage, and we have to admit that we sometimes do, give us the grace of remembrance; help us to remember the beautiful day when we vowed our love for each other, in good times and in bad, in sickness and in health. Help us to remember that on our wedding day it was not only we who promised to be faithful to each other, but also You who promised to be faithful to us. We know we can always depend on You to help us get through the difficulties of life. Loving Father, teach us to live our covenant vows the way Your Saints did—by giving our all, including our own lives, for love of You and Your people. Help us also to remember all who were present at our wedding—the wedding party, the minister, and all of the guests who came to support us on our special day. May we remember our responsibility to be a living sign and a true witness to the vows we exchanged that day, a commitment, we pray, that will last forever! We ask this through Christ our Lord. Amen.

DINING TOGETHER

Suggested Menu: Grilled Chicken with Mango (or fresh fruit) relish, Herbal Orzo pasta, and Pan-roasted Zucchini. Dessert: Peaches and Cream.

Sweet and sour fresh fruit relish—like mango, or even seasonal peaches and apricots—offers a great compliment to any grilled meat, including chicken marinated in buttermilk, with a hint of heat from your favorite hot sauce. The flavors are reminiscent of Pacific Island cuisine. Add some Mediterranean herbs to soft Italian orzo pasta, and you have a dish that brings two different romantic settings together on one plate! End your meal with the elevated and comforting flavors of peaches and cream.

GRILLED CHICKEN

1 cup	buttermilk
2 Tbsp	your favorite hot sauce
2	6-8 oz chicken breasts, filleted to create a total of 4 equal-sized pieces
1 tsp	salt
1 tsp	pepper
1 tsp	garlic powder
2 Tbsp	olive oil

Pour buttermilk and hot sauce into a glass or plastic bowl. Season filleted chicken breasts with salt, pepper, and garlic powder. Put chicken breasts in buttermilk mixture for at least 15 minutes, maximum 30 minutes. When ready to cook, brush olive oil onto a grill pan or nonstick skillet. Remove chicken from the buttermilk, and lightly dab both sides of the chicken with a paper towel to soak up excess buttermilk. Discard buttermilk mixture. Place on the hot skillet. Sear chicken breasts for 2 minutes over high heat. Reduce to medium heat, and continue to cook the chicken for another 2–4 minutes. This cooking process allows you to create the eye-pleasing "grill marks" on the chicken. Flip chicken, and cook for another 3–5 minutes or until chicken is fully cooked. Remove chicken, place on a plate, and let the meat rest for about 5 minutes, before plating and cutting.

MANGO (OR FRESH FRUIT) RELISH

1	mango, peeled and diced (substitute: peaches or apricots)
2 Tbsp	red wine vinegar
2 Tbsp	olive oil
4 tsp	fresh chopped cilantro
2 Tbsp	red onion, minced
1 tsp	salt
1 tsp	pepper
2 tsp	lime juice

Peel mango (or substitute to fruit), cut into ⅛ inch cubes, and place in a bowl. Add vinegar, olive oil, cilantro, red onion, salt, pepper, and lime juice. Gently mix ingredients together. Set aside in refrigerator, until ready to serve. To serve, scoop 1–2 tablespoons of relish over the warm grilled chicken.

HERBAL ORZO

1 cup	dried orzo pasta
4 cups	water
2 Tbsp	butter
1 tsp	salt
½ tsp	garlic powder
½ tsp	dried oregano
½ tsp	dried thyme
½ tsp	dried parsley
2 Tbsp	Parmesan cheese

Boil water in a small pot. Add orzo. Cook according to instructions. When cooked, drain excess water, leaving about 1 tablespoon of water in the pot. Add butter, salt, garlic powder, oregano, thyme, and parsley, and mix together. Add the Parmesan cheese, and mix together, until cheese is completely melted and creamy.

PAN ROASTED ZUCCHINI

1 med	zucchini
2 Tbsp	olive oil
1 tsp	salt
1 tsp	pepper
1 Tbsp	dried oregano
1 tsp	garlic powder

Cut the zucchini lengthways to create four fillets. Combine the rest of the ingredients in a small bowl, and mix until fully incorporated into the oil. Brush both sides with flavored oil. Place on heated grill pan for 2–3 minutes on one side. Carefully flip to cook for 1 more minute on the other side. Carefully remove and set aside before plating.

PEACHES AND CREAM

2	peaches, peeled and sliced into sections
1 Tbsp	lime juice
¼ cup	sweetened condensed milk
¼ cup	evaporated milk
1 tsp	mint, finely minced for garnish
optional	2-4 sugar cookies, (store-bought or homemade)
optional	slice of lime for garnish

Peel and cut peaches into sections. Place in a bowl. Add sweetened condensed milk lime juice and evaporated milk. Gently mix together. Place in the refrigerator, and chill for about half hour before serving. Then stir again, and dress up desserts with a slice of lime, a crumble of your favorite sugar cookies, and a sprig of mint leaves. You can also serve this as a warmed dish by simply heating the contents in a small saucepan over medium heat. Before it starts to boil, remove from heat, and serve with a few crumbles of your favorite sugar cookie.

Cooking Tip:
Fresh fruit makes for a delicious and beautifully presented dessert. Use your creative cutting skills to make designs of fruit on your plate, or use skewer fruit, and place in a long glass of sauce for a dramatic and fun dessert presentation.

GROWING TOGETHER

Write out a few ideas, thoughts, or prayers on how this chapter can strengthen your marriage.

_____
_____
_____
_____
_____
_____
_____
_____
_____
_____
_____
_____
_____
_____
_____
_____
_____
_____
_____
_____
_____
_____
_____
_____
_____
_____
_____
_____

Chapter 5

The Honeymoon is Over

The Reality of Forgiveness

> *Therefore, putting away falsehood, speak the truth, each one to his neighbor, for we are members one of another. Be angry, but do not sin; do not let the sun set on your anger, and do not leave room for the devil... [And] be kind to one another, compassionate, forgiving one another as God has forgiven you in Christ.*
>
> EPHESIANS 4:25–28, 32

At one point in most couples' lives, they were the happiest two people in the world! If a marriage isn't rooted in the Eternal—the One, Good, Beautiful, and True—that happiness can easily slip into misery, and it doesn't take very much for that to happen.

Just consider the realities of everyday life: a spouse has a few tough days at work and inevitably comes home irritated. One of the spouses feels neglected if the other spends a few too many late nights out with friends. Sprinkle in a few disciplinary issues with the kids, a few nagging comments from the in-laws, and a missed anniversary and voilá! It's a recipe for disaster!

When the bad times come along, it's easy for spouses to wonder, "Why did I marry this person?"

If your marriage ever gets to the point where it feels like all is going wrong, keep hope! God sealed your wedding day promises; He still wants you to love each other with His love, and He can help you do just that. God reminds us that those inevitable disagreements do not have to end in divorce. In fact, if couples properly use effective communication techniques, then disagreements don't even need to turn into fights, much less separation. If separation does become necessary, however, that doesn't mean that the marital bond has been torn asunder. Again, there is always hope.

Restoring harmony in a marriage, within a Christian framework, is possible because God made reconciliation a sacrament. This means that making up and getting back together again is a reality established by God Himself! In fact, God not only suggests reconciliation, He *commands* that it occur, especially between people who have vowed to love each other "until death do us part." This means that even the nastiest arguments can be lovingly resolved if the marriage is rooted in God's forgiving love.

Reconciliation, however, often must be preceded by some reminders about fidelity. It also requires the couple to learn, or perhaps remember, some effective and loving communication skills.

As the previous chapter established, spouses do not promise *perfection* to one another on their wedding day; rather, they vow *faithfulness*. No one but God can claim perfection, and those disputes that stem from our human imperfections require spouses to respond with precisely what they promised on their wedding day—faithfulness—despite their spouse's (and their own) faults.

Though it takes a certain level of maturity to do this, spouses must remind themselves often that just because their marriage has its share of irritations and frustrations, it doesn't mean they don't love each other.

Even couples that argue frequently aren't necessarily on the fast track to a divorce. In fact, those couples that persevere through their struggles actually become a powerful witness to the love that they have for each other. They may just need to learn how to love each other better and communicate their love more concretely.

After a serious fight, some couples feel tempted to question, "Does my spouse still love me?" In faith, they need to realize that the answer to this question was given on their wedding day when they vowed *faithful love* to one another.

The better question to ask is, "How can I love my spouse, even if he or she doesn't act lovingly toward me?"

The type of marital problems I'm addressing in this chapter refers to the typical struggles that nearly every couple faces: repeated disagreements, arguments and sometimes what feels like irreconcilable differences, etc. I am not, however, talking about abuse—either physical or emotional. I cannot say enough about the dignity of marriage, which requires that spouses treat each other as gifts from God.

Unfortunately, violence in marriage sometimes occurs, contradicting the marriage vows and committing a crime against human dignity. Here I must offer some fatherly advice: If there is physical abuse, psychological abuse, or harm to

 ## TALKING TOGETHER

- What are the best conversations you've ever had with each other?

- Do you remember your first big fight when you were dating? What was it about and how did it get resolved?

- When you were children, do you recall times when your parents got into arguments? If you could turn back the hands of time and offer them counsel, direction, or advice, what would it be?

- Have you ever heard this advice given to a husband or wife who is going through a difficult time: "You have to do what's best for you"? Do you agree with that statement? Would more accurate advice be, "You have to do what's best for the both of you" or "you have to do what's best for your family"? Which advice is best?

- Can you relate to the story at the end of this chapter? Are there things that you do that may annoy your spouse, even if you never intended to create that frustration? What are they, and have you discussed them in order to be more loving and less annoying?

- What is the most romantic or most memorable way you've made up or said, "I'm sorry"? Did it make your love sweeter than before?

- How would you interpret the passage, "Never let the sun set on your anger"? What are some practical ways to follow that biblical advice?

- How is God's love different than human love? How do you try to love each other—humanly or Godly?

the point where a spouse fears for their security, the victim should seek immediate distance, safety, professional help, and if necessary, legal or police protection. Desperate situations such as these require a firm pastoral response accompanied by prudence.

During a wedding ceremony, I once heard a Monsignor offer sage advice to a newly married couple—the same words you read at the beginning of this chapter, "Do not let the sun set on your anger." The wisdom of this advice is very clear: when you get into an argument, try to make peace in your heart before you go to bed at night, even if you can't bring yourself to make-up or apologize from the heart, and even if you have to sleep in separate beds! If each spouse, as an act of will, simply prays for God to grant restful and peaceful sleep to the other, the discussion is likely to continue the next day in a healthier and more productive way.

Spiritual theology affirms that evil in this world desperately tries to separate what God has united, but God forbids anyone—human or spiritual—to destroy what He has joined. Even so, a couple can give permission to evil, opening themselves up to the temptation to separate when struggles occur. This permission can result in a spiritual suicide for the marriage.

How often spouses place themselves in temptation's way by lying, cheating, or stealing! Underestimating the power of true love—a love that can forgive and heal—is just one side of the coin; the flip side is underestimating the power of evil and losing sight of the fact that it will stop at nothing in its effort to destroy this love. That evil, and not paying heed to it, can lead to petty bickering, arguments, and all-out fights.

Spiritual battles must be engaged with an arsenal that includes spiritual weapons. When couples take the time to reflect and pray about how they got into an argument in the first place, oftentimes they discover that it started off as something small that somehow managed to grow into something seemingly insurmountable. Honest and regular communication is the key to preventing relatively petty matters from becoming bigger. Regular prayer—talking with God and each other—is the best form of communication to help a couple overcome the temptations placed in their path by evil.

Couples who pray together on a regular basis necessarily become more open and honest with each other, because they know that a lie to their spouse essentially means lying to God—the "Third Person" in the marriage covenant. Some may think they can get away with a "little white lie" to a spouse, but the one Person they can never lie to is God.

That is why prayer helps couples avoid finger-pointing and instead moves them to humbly accept responsibility for their own (and one another's) faults and failures. When a spouse prayerfully concludes, "This is my fault," it can lead to the humility that's necessary to say, "I am sorry. I love you." On the other hand, when a spouse prayerfully discerns innocence, God can give that person the patience and strength to say, "I forgive you, and I love you."

Spouses who truly love one another find themselves seeking and giving forgiveness regularly throughout their marriage. That kind of give-and-take is a crucial part of every good marriage; saying things like, "Please forgive me," and "I forgive you," are just some of the multifaceted ways that we can say, "I love you." After all, isn't forgiveness God's way of expressing love?

As important as it is for couples to invest great energy and time into prayer, both personally and communally, spouses must resist the temptation to "hide behind their piety," so to speak, by trying to "pray their troubles away," without also taking further action. When a couple engages in sincere prayer during times of struggle, God will put in their hearts a certain direction in which to go to carry out a practical plan for reconciliation.

It's important for couples experiencing difficulty to realize that they're not alone. Talking with the priest or minister who blessed your ceremony is a great place to begin looking for help. Faith-based counseling services can also provide direction that can improve a couple's ability to communicate. Even retreat experiences can give a struggling couple a forum in which to learn improved communication skills and a deeper understanding of their problems. Local parishes usually have available resources to point couples in the right direction.

It's also a good idea to consider speaking with the official wedding witnesses—the best man and maid or matron of honor. Remember, these special people promised to pray for and encourage the couple as they went forth from their wedding day to fulfill their vows of lifelong faithfulness. Having a prominent place in the ceremony, so close to the couple, these people will no doubt remember that image of two people very much in love with each other. They may be able to help put into perspective any problems they're experiencing by reminding them of the powerful prayers that they uttered on their wedding day. Yes, faithful (not perfect) couples know that help is only a prayer away!

Couples should avoid any advice-giver who will simply encourage an easy way out, like legal separation. We usually know who they are. Rather, seek the advice of people who have demonstrated their own faithfulness, especially those who have persevered through many years of marriage.

While a perfect, quick-fix solution isn't usually available, there are people who want your marriage to be a powerful image of exactly what it is: indissoluble. Find them, and ask for their prayers and advice.

All good marriage counseling services have a similar underlying objective: to help couples communicate more honestly, lovingly, and regularly. That kind of communication takes practice, and a few simple exercises can help.

One such exercise begins by having spouses make a list of all of the positive traits about the other, then saying a prayer and thanking God for these attributes slowly, deliberately, and one at a time. Participants in this exercise are instructed to allow these positive traits to penetrate both heart and mind, just as they did when the couple got married.

Next, the spouses are asked to make a list of the things that frustrate or anger them about each other. Once again, time is taken to reflect and pray about each of these issues slowly and carefully. The spouses are instructed to ask God to reveal to them "the bigger picture."

Reflecting on their spouse's traits in this order, along with prayer, provides the perspective necessary to see the other's faults in the light of all their positive attributes. Taking time to pray about the good and the bad also gives a couple much-needed time to help heal any of the immediate hurts (i.e., it avoids those knee-jerk reactions that can compound matters). In this regard, time in prayer heals many wounds.

For example, a husband may feel like his wife nags him about household chores, but prayerful reflection may humble him enough to admit to some tendencies toward procrastination or laziness. On the flip side, the wife might prayerfully learn to accept that her husband isn't really a *bona fide* couch potato but simply fatigued from his long days at the office. Prayer—our conversation with God—teaches us how to discern faults and empowers us to seek and grant forgiveness.

Another prayerful communication exercise is one in which couples are asked, "What about your spouse would you like to change?" A closely related follow-up urges participants to consider, "What about myself would my spouse like to change?"

Prayerful and reflective conversation can help spouses to see that changing the other person first requires a change in their own perspective and understanding. This is a great reminder that we're all in need of change. Again, no one but God is perfect. Yes, change is possible and sometimes necessary, but it can take time. This would be a good time to recall that famous Bible passage from St. Paul's letter to the Corinthians, "Love is patient, love is kind…" (1 Cor. 13:4)

Our weak and broken humanity, sprinkled with a few temptations from the Great Deceiver, constantly challenges God's faithfulness but cannot prevail. God is truly in love with humanity—He bears us, forgives us, and provides us with countless opportunities for forgiveness. God's love for humanity perfectly models the type of love promised by married couples. Therefore, spouses cannot thrive by loving each other in a worldly way; rather, they love in a Godly way, with holiness—patiently, kindly, humbly.

A prayerful conversation with God can help spouses learn a great deal about themselves and their default behaviors when faced with an interpersonal challenge. For instance, does a spouse clam up or blow up during a disagreement? Do challenges lead to tears and running away, or is anger and aggressive confrontation more the norm? None of these reactions are helpful, of course, but oftentimes the people who engage in them don't even recognize these tendencies in their own behavior. Needless to say, this is often step one on the path to better communication.

During my homily for the wedding ceremony, I sometimes ask, "Does anyone in the congregation have perfect advice to ensure that this couple will never have any problems or big fights?" No one has ever raised a hand!

While no person can provide "perfect" advice, there is plenty of good advice for those who encounter problems like the things we discussed—personal prayer, prayer as a couple, asking for or giving forgiveness, seeking the help of experts to help you stay faithful, etc.

There are countless resources available for spouses who want to improve their relationship by sharpening their communication skills. All that is required is for couples to take up these resources while seeking from God the grace and strength necessary to put the information into practice. Consider this chapter a personal invitation for couples to do just that and to talk about it together on a dinner date!

I'd like to conclude by sharing a story that emphasizes the need for good communication around the dinner table. It's a perfect *Grace Before Meals* ending!

There was a couple married for almost 50 years. Each week, the husband would make his wife a sandwich using the two end pieces of the loaf. This annoyed the wife, but she never said anything about it. Well, this sandwich-making practice went on for years and years until one day, after praying for strength, she finally offered her frustration to her husband.

"For almost 50 years, you've used the end pieces of the bread to make my sandwich. I never asked for those end pieces, nor do I even like them. Why do you insist on giving this to me every week?"

The husband sheepishly responded, "I'm so sorry. I should have asked you. Those end pieces are my favorite pieces. I wanted to give you what I thought was the best part."

What a great lesson in communication!

When the honeymoon ends and reality hits, will couples rely on their own strength to get through their problems? They can try, but they must remember that humanity is imperfect, and it is usually that lack of virtue that got the couple into trouble in the first place! A far better approach is to rely on God's strength and follow His example of love and forgiveness.

With God's Grace, couples can experience mini-honeymoons through the simple act of honest communication—the kind that makes God's patience and mercy present to one another. Speaking the truth to each other can set a couple free to renew those wedding day promises. When spouses forgive each other as God forgives, they will more fully understand, practice, and live the love they promised in good times and in bad. When they make up, they will see their love transformed into something eternal, good, beautiful, and true!

PRAYING TOGETHER

It's recommended that an Act of Contrition—a prayer like the one to follow—should be recited every night before going to bed. While there are many ways to express a contrite spirit in prayer, there must always be the following elements in order to receive God's forgiveness: (1) We admit that we did wrong. (2) We humbly ask forgiveness for the specific faults we've committed. (3) We resolve to try to do better and avoid the things that lead us to sin. The spirit and the words of this prayer can help couples make amends and prevent them from turning small disagreements into big fights. Perhaps it's a prayer that couples can pray together every night, before the setting of the sun.

Let us pray: God, you know how weak we are. We struggle to be good for each other and to be good for You. When we fall, when we make mistakes, and when we consciously sin against You and our spouse, help us to be mature and responsible enough to seek forgiveness. Help us to be quick to forgive each other, knowing that You will forgive as we forgive. Lord, giver of peace, help us to learn better ways of dealing with our problems prayerfully, and if necessary, through the guidance of other faithful couples or even professionals. We pray for couples that struggle in their marriage. May our relationship be a good example of what it means to be forgiving and faithful. With our prayers, words, and gestures may we show to the world Your love working in our marriage. We ask this through Christ our Lord. Amen.

 # DINING TOGETHER

Suggested Menu: Sweet Potato Shepherd's Pie and Mixed Green Salad.
Dessert: Bananas Foster

Some foods immediately bring comfort to the soul. Shepherd's pie is definitely one of those dishes. This unique spin celebrates a fusion of flavors from rustic American sweet potato, savory meats, and bubbly melted cheddar cheese for a sharp contrast. An easy side salad with a fresh dressing brightens the flavors, cleanses the palate, and prepares any couple for an exciting dessert to flambé!

SWEET POTATO SHEPHERD'S PIE

2 large	sweet potatoes (approximately 2 cups potatoes)
1 Tbsp	butter
2 tsp	cane sugar (substitute: brown sugar, but it darkens the bright orange color of the sweet potato in the cooking process)
¼ cup	chicken broth
1 Tbsp	olive oil
2	Italian sausages (mild or hot), casing removed
¼ lb	ground beef
¼ lb	ground veal or turkey
1 clove	garlic, finely minced
1 tsp	ground sage
1 tsp	salt
1 tsp	pepper
¼ cup	white wine
2 cups	frozen mixed vegetables
¼ cup	white cheddar cheese, grated

Poke sweet potatoes with a fork about 5–6 times around the spud. Cook potatoes in microwave oven for 8–10 minutes, high heat. When the potato is cooked, use a towel to remove and let cool. Once cool, cut each potato in half, and use a spoon to scoop out the potato into a bowl. Discard the skin. Combine butter, sugar, and chicken broth into the same bowl, and put in microwave for 1 minute. Or place these same ingredients in a small saucepan, and heat until they begin to simmer. Once the butter is completely melted, gently mash or whisk together until the potato is the desired consistency. It should be similar to mashed potatoes. Set aside, and prepare the meat portion of the dish.

Meat preparation: Heat olive oil in a pan. Add sausage, ground beef, and ground veal or turkey to pan, and cook for about 2–4 minutes or until the pinkness is almost gone. Use wooden spoons to break up the sausage meat for more consistent pieces. Season meats with garlic, sage, salt and pepper. Add ¼ cup of white wine, mix together, and allow this to cook for approximately 2–4 minutes. Add frozen vegetables and mix together, until the vegetables are fully incorporated and cooked to desired softness. Since the meal will still be cooked in an oven, it's recommended that you not overcook the meat or frozen vegetables.

Assembling shepherd's pie: Preheat oven to 350 degrees. Apply a nonstick spray to an oven-safe square pan. Use half of the sweet potato mixture, and cover the bottom the pan, using a spatula to make it an even spread of potato. Drain the meat and vegetable filling before placing on top of the sweet potato. Top off the meat with the rest of the potato mix. Grate ¼ cup of white cheddar cheese over the entire top of the pan. Put in oven for 8–10 minutes or until the cheese is melted and bubbly. Remove and let cool 5 minutes before serving.

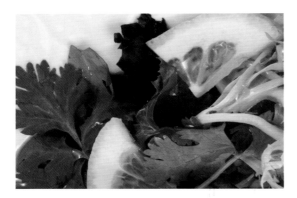

MIXED GREEN SALAD WITH HERBAL CITRUS DRESSING

½ bag	prewashed mixed field green lettuce or your preferred lettuce
1 Tbsp	olive oil
1 Tbsp	lemon juice
¼ tsp	salt
¼ tsp	black pepper
¼ tsp	dried thyme
¼ tsp	dried oregano
¼ tsp	onion powder

Whisk together olive oil, lemon juice, salt, pepper, thyme, oregano, and onion powder in a bowl. When ingredients are fully mixed together, refrigerate until ready to use. Pour over greens, and toss together. Serve immediately.

BANANAS FOSTER

2 Tbsp	butter
½ cup	brown sugar
½-1 cup	spiced rum
2	bananas, peeled and cut in ¼" pieces
½	lemon, juiced
2 sprigs	mint
	whipped cream
optional	Scoop of vanilla ice cream, 2 sugar cookies, or 2-4 lady fingers for something crunchy

CAUTION: this recipe can cause flames. Be sure to keep your distance when cooking with alcohol. Be sure to remove any other flammable objects near and above the stove. Have a lid large enough to cover the pan, as well as a fire extinguisher in case accidents occur.

Heat nonstick skillet, and melt butter and sugar together over low flame. Mix until fully incorporated. To flambé, carefully add spiced rum to the pan. Move pan to the side of the burner, and slightly tilt the pan over a flame, careful not to spill any of the rum. This slight tilting exposes the fumes of the rum to the stove's flame which will immediately cause a burst of fire. Place the pan in its normal position over the heat, and let the ingredients cook together, until fire diminishes. Or, to flambé, use lighter with an extended pointer. To avoid the flames, turn down the heat to low, and let the ingredients simmer together, avoiding any exposure to the stove's direct flames. Cook for about 1–2 minutes. Immediately add bananas and lemon juice to the pan, and mix together, until bananas begin to soften. Serve in a small bowl with some of the juices.

Option: Place two sugar cookies or four ladyfingers on the bottom of the bowl, served with a scoop of ice cream. Garnish with a dollop of whipped cream and a sprig of mint.

Cooking Tip:
If you are uncomfortable with a flaming pan, use a separate saucepan to heat the rum over medium heat, and allow to cook for 5 minutes or until it starts to boil. Remove from heat carefully, and pour over sugar and butter combination. There is still a chance the alcohol will catch fire, but it will be contained to a small saucepan and will not spread with the butter combination. And if flames ignite, be sure to have a lid to cover up and smother the flame. Always remain calm, confident, and prepared.

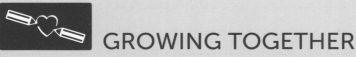

GROWING TOGETHER

Write out a few ideas, thoughts, or prayers on how this chapter can strengthen your marriage.

_____

_____

_____

_____

_____

_____

_____

_____

_____

_____

_____

_____

_____

_____

_____

_____

_____

_____

_____

_____

_____

_____

_____

_____

_____

Chapter 6

Loving In God's Law the In-Laws

Stretching Our Love to the Extended Family

> " *Moses went out to meet his father-in-law, bowed down before him, and kissed him. Having greeted each other, they went into the tent. Moses then told his father-in-law of all that the Lord had done to Pharaoh and the Egyptians for the sake of Israel... Then Jethro, the father-in-law of Moses, brought a holocaust and other sacrifices to God, and Aaron came with all the elders of Israel to participate with Moses' father-in-law in the meal before God.* "
>
> EXODUS 18:7–8, 12

God's Law of Love is: Love one another as I love you. For married couples, this law begins to take on newly profound meaning on their wedding day.

In helping couples prepare, I make sure they know that their invited guests are not mere spectators assembling to watch a show. Rather, the entire congregation is called to actively participate in the ceremony by offering prayers on their behalf.

I like to invite couples to consider taking a moment during the ceremony to place flowers before a statue or an image of the Blessed Virgin Mary as a gesture of veneration and as a symbolic way of requesting prayers of intercession, not just from the Queen of Heaven, but from all those in heaven.

I let them know that in many wedding ceremonies that I've witnessed, the cantor will begin singing a beautiful rendition of the classical "Ave Maria" as this is taking place, at which point all the handkerchiefs come out!

In spite of the inevitable tears, it's an occasion of great joy for the wedding party and guests to witness the couple's faith in the power of prayer and this concrete expression of their confidence in the value of the prayers offered on behalf of Heaven, particularly those of the Blessed Virgin Mary who is "full of grace."

Almost every couple that I've prepared for marriage, after taking some time to consider how intercessory prayer can strengthen their commitment to one another, has freely chosen to incorporate this beautiful floral offering into the ceremony without reservation. Well, maybe just one reservation.

Many couples realize that their non-Catholic guests may not fully appreciate the concept of "prayers from Heaven" until it is explained. I let the couple know that prior to the floral offering, I will speak to the congregation about the importance of seeking the prayerful support of those who love us (something nearly everyone already does), and I'll encourage the couple, in front of the assembly, to request prayers from their family members and other invited guests. I will also ask them to remember to seek the prayerful intercession of those special people who are no longer with us here on Earth but who we pray are in Heaven looking down upon us.

Having witnessed many inter-religious weddings, I also know that some Christians have been taught to think of our Marian prayers as especially incompatible with the adoration that is due to Christ alone. I simply explain that this gesture toward Mary and the Saints is not unlike seeking prayers from family and friends, only in this case, we are seeking prayerful intercession from those who dwell in Heaven, those whom all Christians believe are even nearer to Jesus and, therefore, more alive than we are!

After listening to this brief explanation, most of the people present (Catholic and non-Catholic alike) come to a deeper appreciation and understanding of the Communion of Saints as our extended family, as well as the responsibility that all present have served in helping the newly-married couple remain faithful to their wedding vows.

The bride's gown, the groom's tuxedo, a handsome ring bearer, and an adorable flower girl are all beautiful things, but none can even come close to the beauty of a couple beginning their marriage united in faithful prayer, together with the prayers of family members, friends, and the saints who dwell in Heaven!

I also like to encourage the couple to present a flower to their parents and to humbly ask for prayers from each of their mothers, their fathers, and their new in-laws. At this point in the ceremony, I will call the congregation's attention to the story of Moses and his father-in-law, Jethro (as we read in the Scripture passage at the beginning of this chapter), and how Moses asked his father-in-law to offer prayers, holocaust, and sacrifices as a way of blessing his life and the life of his family.

Once again, the tears of joy flow!

This touching moment makes the reality of parental love tangible. Mom and Dad embrace their little girl and then extend a prayerful handshake, hug, or kiss to the newest member of the family, their son-in-law. It's a bittersweet

 ## TALKING TOGETHER

- What are some of your parents' characteristics that are evident in you? Do you like these traits? What are some of the family traits you would rather not have?

- On your wedding day, did you ever consider just how important the extended family is to your marriage? Who was the happier in-law on your wedding day?

- What are some of the ways your in-laws have helped you? What are some ways your extended family relationships can be improved?

- How do you manage the balancing act between the different events and responsibilities of the in-laws? Is it working? Is there any advice you would give to your children, should God call them to the vocation of marriage?

- During your wedding, did you make a dedication of flowers or a similar symbolic gesture? How would you interpret these symbols now?

- Is there a relative or in-law that could use some cheering up? Consider exploring ideas on how to help your in-laws, especially the older and lonelier family members.

- The term "in-law" sounds so negative to some people! If you could use another term to describe your in-laws, what would it be? What do you think of couples who refer to their spouses' parents as mom and dad?

- Have you ever read the Book of Ruth, in which the mother-in-law and daughter-in-law become like blood relatives? Is this something you have or would consider sharing with your own in-laws? If not, why?

moment—saying goodbye to their child while also welcoming another. In faith, we understand this as a blessing from God wherein He helps our families to grow in love as we welcome new members.

This grace-filled moment, in a ceremony that sacramentally joins two people in marriage to "become one flesh" (Genesis 2:24), serves as a powerful reminder that the bride and groom are called to love and respect their new in-laws as each would love his or her own mother and father.

It is true, however, that in-laws by their very nature differ from our own family, and adapting to the idiosyncrasies of this new branch, after so many years of doing things "our way," may come a bit too quickly for some. In this day and age, it seems that people sometimes date for years without ever really getting to know their partner's parents. But developing a relationship with future in-laws during the dating and courtship process can overcome a lot of would-be obstacles. For people who have a Godly love for their spouse or future spouse, becoming more personally familiar with their beloved's parents is a moment of grace—not anxiety.

In today's dating world, when you bring a special person home to meet mom and dad, it's a sign that you're incorporating that person into your family a little bit at a time. Sharing our family is something that helps us to share our true selves.

There's an old axiom: If you really want to get to know someone, meet that person's family and friends. There's a great deal of wisdom to this! Jesus Himself teaches us as much by giving Mary, His Mother, to the children of the Church to call their very own, that she might lead them to a deeper understanding of who He is. Likewise, Jesus chose His closest friends, the Apostles, to be the ones who would reveal His true identity and nature to the world.

Well, the same goes for us, and by developing a loving relationship with in-laws, as well as our spouse's closest friends, we signal a fuller acceptance and desire to know as intimately as possible the person we love.

While it may be true that the husband is married to his wife and not specifically to the rest of her family, he must recognize and embrace the responsibility he has to love, respect, and honor her family for the simple reason that his wife (hopefully) still loves her own family, too. God's Law of Love demands no less—to love one's spouse so much that this love embraces their family too. Rejecting this responsibility is a strong indication of the kind of selfishness and immaturity that eventually leads to problems for the entire family, beginning with the couple.

Unfortunately, it's not difficult to imagine a marriage filled with animosity between spouses and in-laws. This is an all-too-common experience because, sadly, many couples have little connection to their own families. These types of marriages often increase in tension and pain, as time goes by, especially around the holidays. Getting married should never mean a divorce between a parent and child. If marriage is built on the Law of Love, it brings together not just two people but also an entire church full of people!

There is great suspicion upon those who claim to love their spouse but harbor deep dislike for the rest of their spouse's family, and for good reason. This always strikes me as a red flag that there is something very unhealthy about the relationship. It's almost like speaking to the Lord in prayer saying, "Jesus, I love You, but I don't really care much for Your Mother, Your saints, or the other people in Your Church."

Can you even imagine? Of course not. The dysfunction in that prayer is so far from an expression of love that it's easily recognized. If we truly love God, we must love His family! That's His commandment: love one another, as I love you. This seems obvious enough with regard to Jesus and His family, doesn't it? Well, the same should apply when we consider our responsibility toward our in-laws.

While parents have a responsibility to share their son or daughter in marriage, the greater responsibility is on the married couple. The couple begins a new life on their own, but they do not live that life to the exclusion of all others. No doubt it's a fine balancing act for couples to determine where to go to celebrate various holidays, which grandparents will spend more time with the grandchildren, or how much time the couple sets aside for each other one-on-one. There's a lot of extra family demands heaped upon newly-married couples! They really need su pport and understanding—not pressure from pushy in-laws. Talking about these decisions over a nice dinner can help couples maintain the proper balance. (You knew it would come back to eating, eventually!)

As a priest, I often recommend that couples pray with each other and for each other's family. Doing this puts current or potential in-law tensions in their proper perspective—a loving, patient, and compassionate perspective. Couples that are truly united in the Law of Love will not view in-laws as a threat to the marriage but as an opportunity to love their spouse even more. They will honor, with gratitude, the parents who brought their spouse into this world. Isn't the gift of life that the in-laws gave to your spouse reason enough to love, honor, and thank them?

I'm not naïve. I do realize that this is not a perfect world, and there are many issues that couples have to consider when dealing with in-laws. Even though I would prefer to have this particular discussion with couples during their engagement, the lessons contained in this chapter are every bit as useful for couples who have been married for many years. Even those who enjoy good relationships with their spouse's family do well to consider how they might better reach out to in-laws as a sign of their love for their beloved. The parents of married children can also benefit from this discussion by considering how they can better support and encourage their sons or daughters in-law, rather than burdening them.

I know what some of you are thinking, and no, it's not pie-in-the-sky. (Another food reference!) With God's grace, all things are possible!

On a personal note, my brother-in-law makes visits to my parents' house quite regularly to help with handyman work. My sister-in-law always makes sure the grandkids spend equal time with both sets of grandparents. My dad's devotion to my mother's parents is nothing short of inspiring! Thankfully, the in-laws that make up my extended family are close enough that we try to rotate holidays with each other, and we always invite one another to our family's major events. I'm very proud to say that every family event with this extended family always has grace before meals.

I repeat, with grace, all things are possible—even a relationship with in-laws that is the exact opposite of the negative stereotypes so common in the entertainment industry. I've witnessed firsthand, in my own family and in many others, that gaining an extended family through marriage is truly a great gift—especially for those spouses who welcome it as an opportunity to grow more deeply in love with their beloved.

Some of the stereotypes are reality for a number of families today, where "in-law" is viewed as little more than just a title. In these unfortunate cases, clearly the couple has forgotten the Law of Love. If this describes your situation, don't despair. Rather, prayerfully consider the insights offered in this chapter an invitation to embrace, with God's help, His Law of Love.

Sacred Scripture is filled with images of loving relationships among in-laws. The story of Moses and Jethro at the beginning of this chapter is just one of them. Ruth and the profound dedication that she demonstrated toward her mother-in-law, Naomi, also comes to mind.

In-laws also include siblings—brothers-in-law and sisters-in-law. We might also, therefore, consider the example of Jesus and how His understanding of who exactly qualifies as brother and sister has nothing to do with being part of a biological family. He ate with sinners and strangers as a symbolic gesture of welcoming them into His Father's house in Heaven!

The point is this—the biblical understanding of the in-law relationship is very different from the sitcom version so common today, one that is oftentimes characterized as challenging, tumultuous, and in some cases detached and even unloving. There's no reason to resign oneself to anything less than the former.

In-laws are a part of every marriage; the question is how? Will the parents be encouraging and supportive or apathetic and unloving? How will they be treated by their sons and daughters-in-law—like extended family toward whom a responsibility is owed in love or as a burden that is reluctantly carried?

On the wedding day, the couple and the entire congregation are given a wonderful opportunity to pray together as one family! Dedicating flowers to the Blessed Virgin Mary, offering petitions before a statue of the Holy Family, or some other appropriately sacred gesture during the wedding ceremony is an excellent way to invite future in-laws to prayerfully celebrate the love that God has for His family. That said, the opportunities for members of extended families to support one another in prayer certainly don't end there. In fact, the wedding day is just the beginning.

It's never too late, no matter how long you've been married, to ask for prayers from family and friends, and yes, even in-laws, being certain to call upon those who dwell in Heaven as well, so that your love for each other may become a compelling reflection of God's Law of Love.

 PRAYING TOGETHER

Let us pray: Light a candle at the dinner table for unity, deliver some flowers to a Marian shrine or an image of the Holy Family, and pray for your family and the in-laws in God's Law of Love.

Lord, we thank You for your goodness in calling us to grow in the virtue of charity, so that our love for each other as spouses will not be limited to just ourselves but will extend to one another's family and friends as well. This kind of love is not easy for us, Lord, especially since we are weak and broken and often fail to appreciate the differences in others. Yet in Your generosity, You give us the grace to be a light for others through our union as husband and wife—a source of beauty as flowers in a garden. Keep us ever close to Your love as a couple, so that together with You we may fulfill the greatest law of all: to love one another as You love us. We ask this through the intercession of the Blessed Virgin Mary and all the angels and saints—our family in Heaven—through Christ our Lord. Amen.

 # DINING TOGETHER

Suggested Menu: Citrus Sweet and Spicy Bourbon-broiled Salmon served over potato and Vegetable Stir-fry. Dessert: Creamy Orange Lemon Slushy.

Celebrate the unique flavors of seafood with a zesty sauce that cuts through the richness of salmon. An Asian-infused flavor potato stir-fry gives a hash-like quality as a side dish, complimenting the bold flavors of the bourbon. For dessert, a couple could have fun experimenting with the bright, palate-cleansing chill of lemon slushy.

SWEET AND SPICY
BOURBON BROILED SALMON

¼ cup	bourbon
¼ cup	honey
1	orange, zested
1	orange, juiced
2	6-8 oz cuts salmon fillets (skin removed)
1 tsp	salt
1 tsp	cayenne pepper

CAUTION: There is a chance the alcohol from the bourbon can catch fire. Remove other flammable objects from the cooking area. See previous chapter on tips for cooking with flammable liquids.

Preheat oven to 350 degrees. Combine bourbon, honey, orange juice, and orange zest in a saucepan, and cook over medium heat, stirring occasionally for about 10–15 minutes or until it reduces and thickens. Once sauce is reduced and thickens, remove from heat, and cool to room temperature. Season both sides of salmon with salt and cayenne pepper. Prepare a baking sheet with a cookie rack on top. Spray both pan and cookie rack with nonstick spray for easier clean up. In a separate plate, pour some of the bourbon mixture to cover all sides of the salmon. Place filets on top of the cookie rack about 2 inches away from each other. Place salmon in oven, and cook for 10 minutes. After 5 minutes, pour about 1–2 tablespoons of glaze on top of each fillet. Cook for 5–10 minutes more. When salmon is cooked to medium-rare (about 15–20 minutes), remove and let rest for about 5 minutes, before serving.

Rinse and chop all vegetables, so that they are as equally-sized as possible. Heat large nonstick frying pan or skillet with water and oil, and add potatoes. Cook until the water has completely evaporated, stirring occasionally, so that all sides of the potato are cooked and begin to caramelize. Add the rest of the vegetables, and season with salt and pepper. Cook for 2 minutes. Add oyster sauce (or soy sauce) and vinegar, and simmer for 1–2 minutes. Serve salmon steaks on top of vegetables.

POTATO AND VEGETABLE STIR FRY

2 cups	water
2 Tbsp	olive oil
1 med	red-skinned potato, cut in ¼" pieces
1 med	carrot, peeled and diced into ⅛" pieces
¼ cup	snow peas
1 cup	white button mushrooms, sliced
½	white onion, diced
1 clove	garlic, minced
1 tsp	salt
1 tsp	pepper
2 Tbsp	oyster sauce (found in the international section of the grocery store—soy sauce can be used as a substitute)
1 Tbsp	red wine vinegar

CREAMY ORANGE LEMON SLUSHY

1	lemon, zested
1 cup	ice cubes
½ cup	sugar
¼ cup	lemon juice, concentrate
¼ cup	orange juice, store-bought
1 cup	heavy whipping cream
1-2	fresh mint leaves for garnish
optional	orange or lemon slice for garnish

Combine all ingredients, except for the mint leaves, into a blender. Pulse until a slushy consistency. Pour into a flat plastic storage container and place in the freezer for about a half hour, depending on your freezer temperature settings. Remove and use a whisk or a fork to mix, making sure it doesn't freeze solid. The slushy is ready to serve when the consistency is a tightly packed slushy or a loose sorbet. To serve, scoop slushy in a martini or wine glass atop a slice of fresh orange or lemon. Garnish with fresh mint leaves.

Note: Makes about 4–6 servings, so you will have some left to share.

Cooking Tip:
Cooking the salmon or any protein on the cookie rack will allow even cooking, by creating a convection of the hot air that surrounds the food. The baking or cookie rack avoids uneven cooking that comes from "boiling," when the piece of meat or seafood unevenly cooks in the moisture of sauce and natural juices.

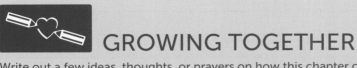

GROWING TOGETHER

Write out a few ideas, thoughts, or prayers on how this chapter can strengthen your marriage.

_____

_____

_____

_____

_____

_____

_____

_____

_____

_____

_____

_____

_____

_____

_____

_____

_____

_____

_____

_____

_____

_____

_____

_____

_____

Chapter 7

Productive Love

Gracing Your Table with the Fruits of Your Love

> *Children too are a gift from the Lord, the fruit of the womb, a reward... Like a fruitful vine your wife within your home, Like olive plants your children around your table. Just so will they be blessed who fear the Lord.*
>
> PSALM 127:3 & 128:3–4

"Where do babies come from?" For many parents, this question brings about an anxiety-filled conversation focusing on storks, birds, or bees. For my dad, a physician, it brought about a mini-course in medical ethics. In some cases, the answers given by unprepared parents can actually leave the young questioner slightly more confused than before; some of them walking away thinking that mommy and daddy don't really know the answer, or if they do, maybe they're just keeping it a secret. For those young people who think their parents are being secretive, it can become their mission to uncover the mystery themselves, sometimes in unhealthy ways!

Needless to say, this age-old question can represent an awkward moment in the lives of both parents and children, but the desire to discover how children are brought into this world is a perfectly natural and beautiful one.

Admittedly, this chapter is going to be one of the heavy ones. It requires couples to put on their thinking caps and consider this dinner as a working meal, where the diners will have to eat, talk, study, work, and hopefully learn—all at the same time. This chapter will require the dinner table to be turned into a desk table—where science, faith, and common sense find common ground.

Even though I'm not a parent, I do know how difficult it is to discuss this sensitive topic. In marriage preparation classes, presenters and the attendees alike can't help but feel a little uncomfortable when talking about sexuality. Though it may surprise you to hear this from a priest, I firmly believe that couples at every stage of marriage should talk about sexuality for what it really is: a gift and a great responsibility.

Think back to what it was like when you returned home from your honeymoon. Do you remember feeling slightly sheepish around your parents? (Trust me: They know what you did on your wedding night!) Despite that childish discomfort, you probably didn't really care what your parents thought. After all, you're married; that makes that act of conjugal love not only 100% okay, but also 100% expected!

Without going too deeply into Church Law, the consummation of the marriage act (sexual intercourse) validates and confirms that marriage is a Sacrament of Union. In the Church's eyes, the sexual act between married couples who engage in it as a sign of self-giving love for each other can be a sign of holiness and faith. Sexuality and faithfulness

TALKING TOGETHER

- If you were trying to explain to a child where babies come from, what would you say? Do you remember how it was presented to you?

- Do you know about or remember the sexual revolution of the 1960s? If you're too young, what have you heard about that tumultuous period of time? What was helpful and unhelpful from that generation?

- In light of the conversation about children as gifts to married couples, have you ever thought about people who want a baby but can't conceive a child? What is your opinion about adoption, and do you think this plays a part in the bigger picture in protecting the gift and sanctity of human life?

- If you ever met a young couple or a young girl facing an unplanned pregnancy, how would you encourage them? Would God be part of your discussion?

- With all of the talk about scientific technology enabling cloning, producing a child in a laboratory, and preventing or terminating a pregnancy, how can you teach your children that life is a gift from God and not just a product of science? Does the Church have any responsibility or role in teaching couples how to approach human sexuality? Which do most couples trust more: scientific progress, social revolution, political groups, or the Church—the place where married couples promised their faithfulness to each other?

- What are the best things about being a parent? Or what do you look forward to the most about being a first-time parent or a grandparent?

- Natural Family Planning (NFP) is a Church-approved method for regulating births without the use of unnatural forms of contraception. It's not the rhythm method but a scientifically proven form of preventing or causing pregnancies, based on honest conversation and a couple's mutual understanding of the woman's natural body. It places emphasis on learning, rather than just doing. Scientific studies, promoted by groups such as Physicians for Life, Human Life International, the Creighton Method, and the Couple to Couple League attest to the method's effectiveness in regulating pregnancy but also improving the qualitative experience of the marital act between the couple. Have you ever looked into any of these studies, and do you think this method could help you and your spouse in planning your family?

- What does it mean to promote the culture of life, to be pro-life, and to uphold the dignity of human life? How do you teach this to your children? How are these teachings contradicted by the world's view of sexuality?

go hand-in-hand. It is no coincidence that when a spouse cheats on the other, we call that person "unfaithful," among many other things! As a priest, I have to make sure that spouses understand that faithfulness means more than just praying together!

I know it's hard for many couples to believe, but the sex act is something God desires to bless. Sometimes, God blesses it with the gift of children. In fact, each time a married couple engages in conjugal love open to that gift, God blesses the couple with a deeper life-giving love for the other. This blessing for the conjugal act simply means that God wants the sexual act among married couples to be fruitful for the marriage. Couples in a Godly marriage aren't supposed to have only romantic love, but also productive love.

At this point of the chapter, couples will have to engage in a more theological, systematic, and deeper investigation of why the Church teaches what it does.

Pope Paul VI's 1968 landmark encyclical, *Humanae Vitae*, brought into the light of day modern theological concepts concerning human life, unborn babies, the false confidence people place in the contraceptive mentality and the evidence of children as God's sacred gift. These would become frank discussion topics for debates throughout the world, even well beyond the Church's walls.

It could not have come at a better time. The Holy Father's discourse confronted the moral relativism of the 1960s head-on in a pastoral letter that reminded men and women of the privileged gift and corresponding responsibility that married couples have as it concerns the transmission of human life. In part, this firm teaching directly responded to the spiritually unhealthy act of contraception, or the interruption of conjugal love, that unfortunately characterized the sexual liberation movement of that time.

Many people expected the birth control pill to be the one-time quick fix that would solve the world's sexual problems and put an end to unwanted pregnancies. The Church prophetically warned that this abuse of technology would actually bring about harm to humanity, and that's exactly what happened. Put simply, the birth control pill broke what did not need fixing in a woman's natural biological composition.

The dialogue about gift and responsibility of marital love inspired by the Holy Father created a firestorm both inside and outside of the Catholic Church family. Various communities that espoused sexual liberation resented the Pope's letter and accused the Church of being "out of touch." It set in motion a strange phenomenon as people began looking at Church leaders as dictators and no longer as pastors upholding the dignity of life. This generation almost forgot that all of the monotheistic religions have historically recognized life as a sacred gift that begins in the womb of the mother. In fact, until recently, all religious groups understood and believed that contraception is morally unacceptable and contrary to the sacred texts of Christians, Jews, and Muslims.

The questions and suspicions concerning this teaching challenged many religiously-minded people, even those who considered themselves to be strong believers.

Modernist thinkers presented the challenge:

How can the Pope tell married couples when to have children? Why is it a sin for a couple to decide for themselves about when they want to have a baby? Why is the Church so concerned about what I do in the privacy of my own bedroom?

These are difficult questions, but the sentiment they express is simply a modern version of the same rebellion that occurred at the base of Mount Sinai, before Moses came down with the Ten Commandments: disobedience, impatience, lack of trust, and, in some cases, downright ignorance. (How many of the people with very strong opinions about the Church's teaching on contraception have ever taken the time to prayerfully read *Humanae Vitae*?)

The Church, once considered a spiritual home, a parental figure, and a friend to the faithful, was now being looked upon as "the enemy of modernity," and so began a confusing trend of contradiction. People continued to come to the Church when they needed a Thanksgiving basket, a compassionate ear, Baptism for their children, a beautiful place to celebrate weddings, or simply a quiet place to seek rest and consolation; at the same time, many people stopped turning to the Church as once they had, in order to be formed in their conscience and moral activity. The fickleness of modernity diminished the relevance of the Church's teachings, while continuing to take advantage of the social benefits it offered.

In *Humanae Vitae*, the Pope, as a spiritual guide, reached out to those who had lost their way to the Heavenly Banquet. He knew that society was being tempted by the junk food of promiscuity. Though the time-tested truths regarding sexual morality may not always be a medicine that's easy to digest, these teachings were precisely the remedy needed by a society that was quickly losing its soul and forgetting about the preciousness and meaning of life.

Opposing groups espoused a "free love" mentality: sexual activity without consequence. Problems are inevitable, however, when couples see sex as something that is self-serving rather than as a selfless act of giving to the other: their spouse, their children, and God.

The Holy Father reminded both individuals and society that all sexual acts have great consequences and social impact. The experience of the past forty years has anecdotally proven him correct: rising divorce rates, sexual abuse, abortion on-demand, senseless murder, euthanasia, a politicizing of morality, etc., are the direct result of society's effort to free itself from the natural laws that govern human sexuality. In spite of these problems, chants for "free love!" continue, even today.

At that confused point in history, the momentary climactic pleasure from the sexual act became the most important goal, diminishing the real goals of sexuality such as commitment, love, responsibility, and selflessness. People sought (and still seek) sexual gratification, even if it meant using other people, willingly or unwillingly. That's what happens when people see sex as a right and not a gift.

Sex even became more important than the child that could potentially come from that act. Sexual gratification became a right that people demanded, rather than a gift that couples gave to each other.

Sadly, society never seemed to recover from this tumultuous period of accepted immorality. Even now, engaged and married couples are still suspicious of the time-honored Church teachings on chastity, purity, and sexual fidelity. The only hope our modern world has for restoring harmony in marriages lies in couples putting these challenging but beautiful teachings about love and responsibility into practice. Yes, only faithful married couples can help restore the dignity of human sexuality!

Couples at various stages of marriage will be challenged to decide whether or not they trust the Church enough to help them with the sometimes difficult issues surrounding human sexuality and bringing forth life (God's children) into this world.

While some would rather kick God out of the bedroom, faithful couples enthusiastically invite God, who is love, more intimately into the inner chambers of their marriage covenant.

As an agent of pastoral care, I realize that some couples fear that talking about sexuality might have a negative impact on romance, but it's important to recognize that romantic feelings and love do not always mean the same thing. Couples in all stages of marriage develop a deeper understanding of the meaning of true love when they discuss sexuality in a mature and faithful way.

In pre-marriage classes, engaged couples are sometimes surprised to find that after a thorough theological discussion about sex, they aren't sexually aroused. Instead, they feel more "sobered up" and detoxified from the pervasive mind-altering lies. So often they have learned about sexuality from agenda-driven schools, skewed media outlets, and even failed relationships. One couple told me that after a very intense discussion about sexuality, they finally felt like grown-ups, ready to accept the responsibility that comes with loving one another! While challenged, they were grateful that the Church still believed in faithful, pure, and committed lovemaking.

Sexual acts are powerful moments in the life of the couple, but as we all know, great power requires great responsibility. In the present case that means taking the time to learn what God teaches about marriage. Think about it—while it may be fun to go scuba diving, no one would even consider entering the water without first learning how to swim. Likewise, no one would ever allow their child to drive a car without first explaining the difference between the gas pedal and the brake pedal. And no one should ever use a gun without proper instruction!

The power of the sexual act requires that people make sure they first know how to love (e.g., swim), respect the body parts that love (e.g., the basic parts of a car), and understand the responsibility that comes from love (i.e., gun safety) before they show their love (e.g., sex in a marriage)! Unfortunately, in some cases, sex is used as a weapon, and in other cases, unbridled sexuality can kill!

The reason sexual relationships in marriage have so many problems is because there is too much doing and not enough understanding. Blessed Pope John Paul II taught millions of married couples about the characteristics of true lovemaking through what is now known as "Theology of the Body," a set of moral teachings given by the Holy Father over the course of more than five years, beginning in 1979. In this interpretation of Christian Doctrine, the Pope articulated in anthropological and modern language the prophetic teaching that Pope Paul VI proclaimed in *Humanae Vitae*, which describes the four characteristics of true sexual love: faithful, free, total, and fruitful.

Clearly, not all sex acts are acts of love: e.g., rape, incest, prostitution, self-abuse, etc. With sex and love so often confused, the Shepherds of the Church have wisely given us a harmonious definition of the sexual act that points to these four attributes as necessary for a truly loving act. These four characteristics serve as pillars that uphold the dignity of the sex act and serve as protection for promised fidelity among the individuals involved in a conjugal act.

Sexual activity as authentic love is always productive. It can sometimes bring about life in the womb, but even apart from this it always produces, at the very least, a deeper love between spouses. When we say that the sex act is productive, this means that it is fruitful and life-giving for the spouses in the total giving of oneself to the other. This can be the case even in advanced age when the activity is confined to simply cuddling. In any event, couples must be open to all of the life-giving effects that are possible in the sexual act, in order for it to be an act of true love.

Love and sex are equal when the married couple expresses and assumes mutual responsibility, and only when the sex act is blessed by God. This statement may sound shocking to many in our culture, but think about it: if we remove faith, responsibility, and the God who is Love from sex, how can the sexual act itself really be called love? When couples experience lovemaking as a holy and Godly act, it is then that they will recognize their offspring as a great privilege and a wonderful gift, not a burden.

Seen in this way, as the Popes have consistently taught, sexuality is a gift from God to His people: it reveals His will for us to be productive in the act of self-giving, so that we may participate in His creative love. God is pro-life because He is pro-creative! His first act was to create the world out of nothing. Jesus' last act of the Eucharist was to create a new heart and new life in His people! When sexual love is characterized as total, fruitful, faithful, and free, a couple will see that children are gifts, and they won't fear or require protection from one another. For loving couples, sexuality becomes a Godly act; children become the fruit of love between mother and father who love each other completely, without reserve.

I realize this chapter was heavy stuff, a plate full of bitter herbs, tasting like medicine. Like a loving parent, the Church and our *Grace Before Meals* movement seek to bring healing to our hurting world, even if the hard truth "hurts" to swallow. But this pill of truth has to be administered. It's much easier to heal the child if the child trusts the loving parent. This chapter, filled with so many facts, needs even more study and reflection. For this reason, I've provided a

few trusted resources for couples to delve more deeply into this ocean of God's merciful love and wisdom.

Our world needs to tell children where they came from, without fear. Go ahead and tell them they are the fruit of mommy and daddy's productive love blessed by God. Tell them how they are cherished blessings that God promised to those who allowed His love into their lives on their wedding day... and on the wedding night.

 ## PRAYING TOGETHER

Let us pray: God, You are the author of all life, human and divine. We share in Your love, which is always creative. At times, we are challenged by the world's view of love, sexual acts, and even human life. Lord, protect us from worldly ways that may infect our marriage. Protect us with the Church's teachings by helping us to deeply understand these truths, through prayer and study, in order to live according to Your will, that we may teach others by our words and example. Father, You know the sins that wounds our marriage. Please forgive us for the times when sex became more about our feelings, rather than an expression of faith. Make us more faithful so that our love can truly be productive each time we offer ourselves to each other. May we truly commit ourselves to You every day as on our wedding day. Bless us with Your love. We invite You into every part of our lives and our homes, including our bedroom. With the prayers of the angels and saints, we ask this through Christ our Lord. Amen.

For more information about NFP, the Theology of the Body, and other resources to better understand the sanctity of human life, check out some of these websites and titles:

http://www.physiciansforlife.org/

http://www.ccli.org/

http://www.creightonmodel.com/

Evert, Jason. *Theology of His Body/Theology of Her Body*

John Paul II; *Man and Woman He Created Them: A Theology of the Body* (Translated by Michael Waldenstein)

West, Christopher. *The Theology of the Body for Beginners*

 # DINING TOGETHER

Suggested Menu: Coconut Curry Creamed Pork Adobo over Seasoned Sticky Rice, with a Cucumber and Carrot Relish. Dessert: Baked Apples stuffed with sweet honey granola.

My mom's version of Philippine pork adobo gets another boost of flavor with curry and coconut cream. Sticky rice soaks up the delicious gravy that mellows and melds the unique flavors together. An easy but fresh salad of carrots and cucumber relish adds color and crunch. A simple deconstructed traditional apple pie is a beautiful way to end this savory meal.

COCONUT CURRY CREAMED PORK ADOBO

1 lb	pork shoulder, cut into ½" cubes (substitute: pork tenderloin)
1 tsp	Chinese Five Spice
2 tsp	curry powder
4 Tbsp	vegetable oil
½	white onion, roughly cut into ¼" pieces
1 clove	garlic, minced
1 tsp	whole black pepper corns (optional, wrapped in a cheese cloth or mesh bag)
¼ cup	apple cider vinegar
¼ cup	soy sauce
1 can	coconut milk (12-13.5 oz)
2	bay leaves

Trim excess fat off the pork shoulder, but keep some marbling of fat in the meat, so that pork stays moist in the braising process. Cut pork into ½ inch cubed pieces. Season with Five Spice and curry powder. Heat vegetable oil in a pot over high heat. Add pork, and sear each piece, approximately 2–4 minutes, stirring occasionally. Add onions, and cook 2–4 minutes or until onions become translucent. Reduce heat to medium. Add remaining ingredients, and continue to cook for 20 minutes in a covered pot, stirring occasionally. After 20 minutes, remove the lid, and cook for another 3–5 minutes or until sauce thickens. Remove the black pepper corn bag and bay leaves, use a small strainer to strain away the whole black pepper corns, or at least caution diners about the whole pepper corns, before serving.

SEASONED STICKY RICE

1 cup	long grain white rice
4 cups	cold water
1 tsp	butter
1 Tbsp	apple cider vinegar
1 tsp	salt
1 tsp	garlic powder

It's best to cook long grain rice in a rice cooker. If you don't have a rice cooker, you can use a large nonstick saucepan. Combine rice and cold water to the saucepan, and cook over medium-low heat. Cook for about 20 minutes, stirring occasionally. It may be necessary to add some water if the rice is still firm after 20 minutes of boiling. However, add only ½ cup of water at a time. When the water has evaporated, the rice should be soft and "sticky." Add butter, vinegar, salt, and garlic powder, and stir together. Serve as a great side dish to any foods with gravy.

CUCUMBER AND CARROT RELISH

1 large	cucumber, peeled
1 large	carrot, peeled
2 tsp	apple cider vinegar
½ tsp	salt
½ tsp	pepper
2 tsp	olive oil

Use a vegetable peeler to make long strips, similar to a flat noodle, for both the cucumber and carrot. Place vegetable shavings in a bowl large enough to contain the ingredients. Add vinegar, salt, pepper, and olive oil. Stir or toss ingredients together. Chill in the refrigerator prior to serving.

GRANOLA BAKED APPLES

1	granny smith apple
¼ cup	water
1	lemon, juiced
2 Tbsp	brown sugar
2 Tbsp	butter
2 Tbsp	balsamic vinegar
½ cup	granola
	Whipped cream

Preheat oven to 350 degrees. Cut the apple in half, from the stem to the bottom core of the apple. Use a melon baller to scoop out the core and seed of the apple, creating a small indent in the apple. Put apples inside a baking dish, core side facing upward. If necessary, slice a small piece off the bottom side of the apple, so that the apple halves rest flat in the baking dish. Add ¼ cup of water to the baking dish. In a separate microwavable bowl or in a saucepan, combine lemon juice, brown sugar, butter, and balsamic vinegar, and heat until brown sugar and butter melt together. Add granola, and mix together. Spoon the mixture atop each apple half, so the apple is completely covered. Bake 30–35 minutes or until the apples are soft. Remove and let cool 5 minutes, before serving with a dollop of whipped cream.

Cooking Tip:
Combining warm, savory foods with a fresh acidic salad gives texture, temperature variety, and an explosion of flavor. This style of eating is quite common in Asian cuisine and is finding quite an audience in the rest of the culinary world, in foods such as cold salads with grilled meats and in refreshing lettuce wraps.

GROWING TOGETHER

Record some of your ideas on how this chapter can help improve your understanding of the Church's teaching of married love and the responsibility of married couples.

_____

_____

_____

_____

_____

_____

_____

_____

_____

_____

_____

_____

_____

_____

_____

_____

_____

_____

_____

_____

_____

_____

_____

_____

_____

Chapter 8

Growing Pains

Raising and Educating Children

> " *Therefore, you shall love the Lord, your God, with all your heart, and with all your soul, and with all your strength. Take to heart these words which I enjoin on you today. Drill them into your children. Speak of them at home and abroad, whether your are busy or at rest.* "
>
> DEUTERONOMY 6:5–7

Where do babies come from? No, you aren't losing your mind and having flashbacks to the last chapter. I simply wanted to explore this innocent question more deeply, moving beyond biology into spirituality.

Children do not only come from mommy's womb; they also come from the knowledge of God's plan working in the hearts and minds of parents. Children are never accidents. Rather, they come from the mind of God and are the product of His wisdom and love!

Children are at once the greatest gift and the greatest responsibility that God gives, not just to parents, but to all of society and, indeed, all the world! It's important that the children in our lives know this, so they may never feel unwanted or unable to recognize the supreme dignity that they possess as beloved members of God's saving plan.

In the Book of Genesis, we read of God's command to people the Earth, but bringing children into this world is only one part of that command. The other consists in subduing the Earth and exercising dominion over the living things that move upon it: e.g. building up the kingdom, a mission that requires parents to raise, nurture and educate their children in the ways of the Lord. In this, the Church understands marriage as a two-fold plan given by God to His people.

"Yes, but what about those couples who do not have children of their own?" you may ask.

Even childless couples have a parental duty: to be an image of parental love by working to build a culture that is welcoming of children and contributing however they may to forming a society that shares in the responsibility of safeguarding our children's well-being. In this way, every couple has a responsibility to help children recognize their personal dignity in very direct, personal ways as with nieces, nephews, the children of neighbors and close friends, etc.

The way parents answer the simple question, "Where do babies come from?" can either help or hinder a child's awareness of the inherent dignity that they possess. As I'm sure you've heard it before, children just seem to have a "sixth sense" that allows them to pick up on an adult's true feelings. This being the case, those married couples who faithfully embrace their vocational responsibility to remain open to the procreative potential of every sex act are naturally well-suited for communicating the truth that children are nothing less than a gift from God. On the other hand, spouses who have adopted the contraceptive mentality which blocks that potential, naturally struggle to do this, even though they may love their own children as much as anyone else.

While one would certainly hope that any child old enough to ask, "Where do babies come from?" will already be well on his or her way to developing a healthy sense of self-worth, the answer given to this particular question can make a lasting impression. In fact, many adults will say that they can remember exactly how their parents answered this question, even if it was many decades ago! This is a great example of the tremendous impact a parent can have on a child by their response to one very simple question.

If parents are ill-prepared to communicate to their child such fundamental Christian truths as the inherent dignity of every human life, rest assured someone else, be it educators in the school system or personalities in the entertainment industry, will step in to influence their young minds, all-too-often, with ideas that contradict the Faith.

Even though our pop culture is full of characters that have a great impact on our children's formation, the Church has always taught that the primary responsibility for educating and forming children rests with parents. The importance of this solemn duty cannot be stressed nearly enough, but we must also recognize it as a great gift.

Educating children is nothing less than participation in the work of redemption! This means that parents are called to cooperate in a unique way with God, our loving Father, and the Church, our wise and Holy Mother. Parenting, when carried out in faith, is a blessing that draws married couples ever more deeply into the very life of God, where they are nurtured by grace and empowered to impart life lessons to their children. From manners to language, from respect to prayers, the formation that children receive in the home is what prepares them for learning in an institutional setting. It also protects them.

 TALKING TOGETHER

- How was your school experience different from what children experience today?

- Who was your favorite teacher when you were in school? Why?

- What was the greatest lesson your parents taught you? What will be the greatest lesson you think your children will learn from you?

- What do you think could improve today's educational institutions?

- Do you know the difference between education and indoctrination? Have you ever experienced the latter? What can you do to prevent it?

- Do you remember your first day of school? Do you remember how you felt? Can you remember how you felt or imagine how you will feel on your child's first day at school?

- Do you remember your first crush when you were in school? Have you ever shared that schoolboy/schoolgirl crush with your spouse?

- Are there any ways that you, as a couple, can be more invested in your children's, grandchildren's, or godchildren's education? If so, when will you take that initiative?

When parents fail to faithfully embrace this obligation, their children enter school unprepared for some of the things they may encounter in the classroom. In far too many school systems, this can include a form of indoctrination at the hands of educators who are eager to promote a pet political agenda: e.g., radical environmentalism, same-sex unions, abortion, and worst of all, relativism.

The classroom isn't the only place where children are exposed to such things. In today's technologically advanced world, danger is lurking just a few keystrokes away. Thanks to PCs, laptops, and smart phones, children have ready access to a virtual universe of decidedly un-Christian content that, all-too-frequently, is deliberately packaged in such a way as to entice young, impressionable minds. Just like the ancient serpent, lies are made deliciously appealing! Parents, therefore, need to be diligent in noting any warning signs that may indicate that their ability to shape and direct their child's personality is being undermined by such outside influences.

It's time for us to admit that our reliance on technology has made family life more difficult, as our society places an increasingly higher premium on developing "friendships" on Facebook, following Hollywood personalities on Twitter and engaging in general online chatter, instead of focusing on the people gathered around our dinner table.

Technological advancements can be used for good, too, of course. Even the Holy See has its own website, and Pope Benedict XVI is the first pope to send messages to the world via a Twitter account! In spite of the fact that technology, both at home and in the classroom, allows people to access useful information almost instantly, it seems that our institutions of higher learning have no room in their curriculum for personal or spiritual formation. Where can a child obtain this kind of education if not from parents? There are some things schools simply cannot provide. Among them are those life lessons that only loving parents have by God-given authority.

Let me be clear: I know many teachers who see their students as extensions of their own human family and are truly dedicated to loving them and raising them to become saintly citizens of Earth on their journey to Heaven. Teachers who approach their vocation in this way deserve to be applauded and supported, even as we never lose sight of the fact that the primary responsibility for the spiritual formation and education of children remains with parents.

Who will teach your children? What will you teach your children? These are definitely dinner conversations that will spice up mom and dad's married life!

Educating children well requires tremendous commitment and sacrifice on the part of the entire family. It's quite possibly the greatest, and perhaps even the riskiest, financial investment a parent makes. Simply paying tuition to a high-priced school doesn't guarantee virtue-filled alumni, and no amount of money can assure that a graduate will actually make use of his or her diploma. Unfortunately, there are other factors: poor choices, bad company, and just plain bad luck, can derail a person's educational dreams. The chances of attaining educational success increase considerably when the process is viewed as a collaborative effort between a loving family, encouraging friends, quality teachers, and an institution that is dedicated to a higher calling.

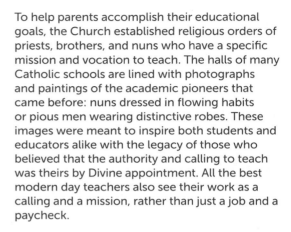

To help parents accomplish their educational goals, the Church established religious orders of priests, brothers, and nuns who have a specific mission and vocation to teach. The halls of many Catholic schools are lined with photographs and paintings of the academic pioneers that came before: nuns dressed in flowing habits or pious men wearing distinctive robes. These images were meant to inspire both students and educators alike with the legacy of those who believed that the authority and calling to teach was theirs by Divine appointment. All the best modern day teachers also see their work as a calling and a mission, rather than just a job and a paycheck.

The Catholic school system, as well as other religious-based educational systems, has a long track record of providing quality education that has consistently earned the respect of many in the academic world. People of faith should be very proud of the history of religious school education. It has been a real hallmark in the development of societies around the world.

In modern times, Catholic identity in education has been put in jeopardy due to the decreasing numbers of nuns, brothers, and priests who have answered the call to devote their lives to educating children. Many religious schools have unfortunately morphed into expensive private schools that are devoid of the rich spiritual formation and classical education that made these institutions so great.

When parents consider school choices for their children, hopefully they will decide on a system or a program that communicates an authentically lived faith and not just a religious name. While most people will say that a solid education is one that will launch their children into a successful career that ultimately leads to financial security, a truly good school is one that cooperates with parents in forming students into virtuous citizens and saints-in-the-making.

Good kids and bad kids come from both parochial schools and public schools, but it's parents who embrace their role as the primary and faithful educators of their children that make the greatest difference. The *Grace Before Meals* movement reminds families that the dinner table, with the help of God's Grace, becomes like a desk in the school that is the family home, the place where some of the most important lessons of life are learned.

For many parents, homeschooling has become a viable educational alternative. Homeschooling has given to society many well-trained, well-educated, and well-mannered young people who strive for success and personal virtue. Many homeschooling families claim that spending this additional quality time together in education has resulted in improved family communication overall. I've seen this firsthand in my own family, as some of my nieces and nephews were homeschooled.

Not all parents are well-suited to homeschooling their children, however. Effective teaching is a skill that must be developed, and parents need to make sure they are truly qualified to teach. When done properly, homeschooling parents can often integrate respect for faith and traditions into the education of children. It's edifying to meet, as I have, impressively intelligent homeschooled children who can hold a normal conversation with their elders while still maintaining the playfulness of a child.

No doubt, homeschooling has had positive effects on some children, but I've also seen the reverse, as children sometimes come to rebel against their parents' over-involvement.

While there are many reasons to homeschool children, there are also risks that might caution against it. Perhaps the greatest concern is that parents, in their desire to protect their children, may inadvertently create a "monastery" or "convent" setting that isolates them from the world. With the amount of time spent together with homeschooling parents, it's easy for the children to become socially awkward and disconnected from the rest of the world. The Church in Her wisdom teaches us that parents are called to serve as the primary, not the exclusive, educators of their children.

To parents who are weighing all of the various educational choices that are available, future parents who are looking into neighborhoods to start a family, grandparents who (thankfully) are involved in their education of grandchildren, and godparents who are meeting their responsibility in helping the parents to raise children in faith, I offer this very important word: balance.

Good education is achieved by a balance in which the parents, who have ultimate control, are an integrated and active part of an educational system that recognizes its boundaries. For parents, this means being involved in school activities, taking time to review homework, and making sure that extracurricular activities are scheduled appropriately. Balance further requires that parents practice what they teach, especially in upholding their own obligation to learn about God through their faithful attendance at Holy Mass and by praying together as a family.

Balance also requires parents to pray for children while they're in school, as well as for the teachers and other school staff, with the hope of creating a true spiritual home in a child's future *alma mater*. In order to maintain balance in a child's education, parents must also monitor school curriculum and textbooks, both in public schools and in religious-based schools.

Seeking to acquire balance urges parents to remain ever aware of their children's friends and classmates. Balanced parents use tact when they talk to a child about his or her friends, especially the ones that are a cause for concern, treating these occasions as an opportunity to teach, rather than a time to judge. Imbalance in this case would be akin to simply locking a kid up in a tower and dictating who can be considered a friend and who cannot. Of course, that's an extreme example, but it helps to illustrate how over-protectiveness leads to nothing good.

Balance is certainly difficult, but it is possible. A good criterion for what constitutes balance is an approach to parenting that allows children to experience true freedom as the fruit of personal sacrifice. This grants a healthy degree of exposure to a wide variety of opinions and ideas, while also providing the faith-filled education they need to make good decisions for

themselves. If this sounds like a high bar to meet, that's because it is. Being a good teacher requires that one first be good a student, a disciple who humbly sits at the Supreme Teacher's feet in prayer!

When growing up, my parents wanted to instill in me three basic life lessons: (1) How to cook and feed myself, (2) How to do my own laundry, and (3) How to balance my finances to ensure that I can live within my means. Of all the practical knowledge my parents imparted, however, the most important thing they taught me was how to pray. This supernatural lesson came in a very natural way. Praying was just what we did as a family. Talking about God was normal dinner conversation.

Faithfulness is what mom and dad taught us by example, in both good times and bad: how they loved one another, how they cared for one another, how they prayed together, and even how they sometimes argued and made up with one another. All of these experiences served as important life lessons for which I continue to thank God. Even my favorite teacher in my favorite class at my favorite school could never teach me what I learned at home. These are the privileged teachings that are reserved especially for "professor parents."

Spouses are called to be faithfully involved in the education of children, especially their own, but the societal obligation, as previously mentioned, belongs to all. If carried out well, children not only learn that mommy and daddy love them, but even more importantly, they discover that God loves them! When that lesson is learned, children become adults who know how to love others as God loves them.

Parents who have imparted this most valuable of lessons naturally have less anxiety about their children's future. Of course, there will always be concerns, but a lively faith will remind them that God's protective presence is with their children at every stage of life, from that first part-time job, to that nervous driver's license test, to the heartache of that first romantic breakup. God is still there after our children graduate, when they marry, when they become parents themselves, and even when they retire. He's there at every turn, consoling them when they fall and rejoicing in their triumphs.

I can understand why some parents are especially proud to say, "My son, the doctor," or "My daughter, the lawyer." I'm also confident that all loving parents are proud, no matter what their child's vocation, whether they wear a white collar, a blue-collar or a priestly collar, like me. When their children are happy, healthy and responsible, parents deserve a healthy sense of accomplishment. They earned it, but imagine the unique joy that comes from being able to say with confidence, "My son is a holy man!" or "My

daughter is loving and faithful!" or "My child is a saint-in-the-making!"

Parents who can do this are to be congratulated for a job very, very well done! And exactly what is the "job description"?

Well, the first thing you should know is that the job isn't truly finished just because the children have reached adulthood. In fact, it doesn't stop when parents are elderly as they continue to educate their children and grandchildren often just by aging gracefully, joyfully, and faithfully and teaching them by quiet example what it takes to get to Heaven.

That's mom and dad's real job. After all, Heaven isn't just where children come from, it is also where they're destined to go!

 PRAYING TOGETHER

Let us pray: All-knowing Father, You gave us the gift of intelligence to master the things of the earth and yet the grace to remain humble in Your presence. You teach us at every moment of our lives as long as we are willing to learn. You give us the ability to communicate so that we can share truth and knowledge with others. You have given us the ability to know, love, and serve You. Lord, when we face a world that does not know You, we know that embracing our vocation faithfully is the only proper response. Father, help us to be good teachers for our children, grandchildren, godchildren, and even to the young people we will encounter in our lives. Give us the determination to be gifted teachers by first being humble students of Your Wisdom and by taking the time to meditate, pray, study, and learn Your ways! Since You give us the ability to learn, give us now the desire to share what we have learned. We also pray for more vocations to the religious orders that once filled schools with dedicated teachers. Bless teachers to be effective, not just by what they say, but by what they do and how they live and love. We ask this through Christ our Lord. Amen.

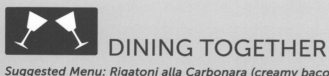

DINING TOGETHER

Suggested Menu: Rigatoni alla Carbonara (creamy bacon and egg pasta) with Fresh Tomato and Olive Bruschetta. Dessert: Tiramisu

This romantic meal comes from the city of romance—Rome, Italy! The unique pasta turns breakfast food ingredients into a luscious gourmet meal. A toasted French bread topped with Mediterranean flavors adds brightness and crunch. The dessert suggestion, tiramisu, which roughly translates to "brings me up" or "turns me up," gives couples a light chocolaty ending to a romantic meal! And with this recipe, you'll have just enough leftovers to keep celebrating with a lunchtime pasta and some dessert to share with friends or your children.

RIGATONI ALLA CARBONARA

½ lb	rigatoni, cooked *al dente*
4 slices	thick-cut bacon, cut into ¼" strips
2	eggs, beaten, plus 2 egg yolks
1 Tbsp	dry white wine (substitute: 2 tsp chicken broth and 1 tsp lemon juice)
1 tsp	salt
2 tsp	pepper
2 Tbsp	butter
½ cup	Parmesan cheese, grated

Boil water in a large pot, and cook pasta according to the instructions on the box. Note: There is no need to add salt or oil to this pasta water. While pasta is cooking, sauté bacon in a large frying pan, until crispy. While pasta and bacon are cooking, prepare the creamy egg sauce by beating together 2 eggs plus 2 egg yolks, white wine (or substitute), salt, and pepper. Beat together until eggs are a smooth consistency. When pasta is cooked *al dente*, drain the water completely, and return the pasta to the pot, but do not return the pot to heat. Immediately add butter and egg mixture over hot pasta, and stir vigorously. The heat of the pasta cooks the eggs into a creamy sauce. Immediately scoop hot bacon, using a slotted spoon, from the grease and add to pasta. Add cheese and stir together. Serve immediately.

Option: Add 1 teaspoon of the hot bacon grease to the pasta. Stir together.

FRESH TOMATO AND OLIVE BRUSCHETTA

1 small	French baguette, cut in half
1 clove	garlic, peeled but kept whole
2 tsp	olive oil
1 large	tomato, diced
⅛ cup	olives (black or green), pitted and diced
1	lemon, zested
1-2 tsp	lemon juice
1 tsp	salt
1 tsp	pepper
1 Tbsp	fresh parsley

Heat griddle or a frying pan over medium-high heat. Cut baguette in half, and lightly brush bread with olive oil. Place facedown in the pan, and cook for about 30 seconds to 1 minute or until the bread begins to toast golden brown. Remove bread from the pan, and immediately rub the garlic clove on top of the bread to give a light garlic flavor. Once the bread has been rubbed, set the bread aside, and discard the garlic clove. In a separate bowl, combine the rest of the ingredients together. Top off each piece of bread with the tomato and olive combination. Garnish with a sprig of fresh parsley.

TIRAMISU

6	egg yolks
1 ¼ cup	white sugar
1 ¼ cup	mascarpone cheese
	(substitute: whip together 6 oz soft cream cheese, ¼ cup butter, ¼ cup whipping cream)
2	12 oz packages ladyfingers
1 cup	very strong coffee (espresso preferred)
1 Tbsp	cocoa powder (sweet or unsweetened)
1-2 Tbsp	store-bought chocolate sauce for decoration
optional	¼ cup coffee-flavored liqueur

Combine yolks and sugar in a non-reactive bowl, and place on a small pot of boiling water. This creates a double boiler, allowing you to cook the ingredients over indirect heat. Cook for 10 minutes, stirring constantly, until the sugar is melted, and the consistency is smooth and silky. Remove bowl from the heat, and add the mascarpone cheese or substitute. Fold ingredients together, until fully incorporated. Set aside. Separate ladyfingers, and line the bottom of a square 8 inch glass baking dish. Combine coffee (and optional coffee liqueur). Brush each ladyfinger with or quickly dunk into the coffee, so the ladyfingers begin to absorb some of the coffee moisture and flavor. Be careful not to let ladyfingers get too mushy. Layer the bottom of the pan with ladyfingers. Scoop ¼–½ cup of cream, and spread over coffee-soaked ladyfingers. Repeat process, until all ladyfingers and cream are used. Be sure the last layer is the cream. Sift cocoa powder on top of the last layer of cream. Chill in refrigerator for two hours. Before serving, drizzle chocolate syrup on plate in any design before plating a scoop of the tiramisu. This recipe serves 4–6 people, so you'll have leftovers later.

Cooking Tip:
If you have leftover pasta, you can simply reheat the pasta by adding some water and oil or butter into a pan. Once it begins to simmer, add the pasta, and cook until the pasta naturally breaks apart and warms through. This method of reheating is much better than microwaving leftover pasta.

GROWING TOGETHER

Record some ideas, memories, or prayers from this chapter that can help you strengthen your own marriage and your commitment to being effective and loving teachers for the younger generation.

_____

_____

_____

_____

_____

_____

_____

_____

_____

_____

_____

_____

_____

_____

_____

_____

_____

_____

_____

_____

_____

_____

_____

Chapter 9

For Richer or Poorer

Money Can't Buy Love

> *No one can serve two masters. He will either hate one and love the other, or be devoted to one and despise the other. You cannot serve God and mammon... So do not worry and say 'What are we to eat?' or 'What are we to drink?' or 'What are we to wear?' All these things pagans seek. Your heavenly Father knows that you need them all. But seek first the kingdom [of God] and his righteousness, and all these things will be given you besides.*
>
> MATTHEW 6:24–26, 31–33

Technically, it doesn't cost anything to be married; remaining married, on the other hand, is another story! When a couple gets engaged, they soon begin calculating just how much the wedding day will cost in dollars and cents. A common question that priests are asked by couples or by the parents who are paying the bill is, "How much does it cost to get married?"

The answer is "nothing and everything!"

Obviously, one of the things I need to let couples know is how much it will cost to use the church building, and you wouldn't believe the negative reactions I sometimes receive when they discover that paying a usage fee is even necessary. It's truly baffling! Some people must not realize that the church building, just like a family's home, requires costly upkeep; things like maintenance, electricity, and personnel are needed to keep it running. Even though the actual fee varies from place to place, I can tell you that it's always far less than the cost of renting even a modest reception hall.

When you stop to consider what you really get in return, the importance of what happens in the sacred space that is the church makes the cost to use it not just a wise investment but a ridiculously great bargain! Unfortunately, I'm no longer surprised to discover that a couple is happy to pay thousands of dollars for a five-hour reception, but is disturbed by

the idea of investing time and money, either by a relatively small church donation or the requirements associated with the Church's marriage preparation program. Even though we know that money can't buy love, happiness, or peace, it does seem that the materialistic, worldly mentality often urges people to bargain for cheap imitations.

Equally baffling to me are the sometimes strange reasons why people choose to get married in a church in the first place. The reasons range from a pretty backdrop for photographs to the church's proximity to the reception hall. I'm always relieved when a couple says something about faith (go figure!) as their reason for wanting a church wedding.

Now, with all of that said, let's not kid ourselves: getting and staying married costs a lot of money! It's important to realize that where a couple's money goes ends up contributing a great deal to the relative stability of their marriage.

Beyond the care of children, a discussion about money is the next priority. I often tell couples that having this discussion with Almighty God (i.e., praying about their money matters) can help them put the "almighty dollar" in its proper perspective!

There's a Filipino wedding tradition, influenced by Catholic Spaniards, that offers great insight into the real value of money in a marriage. In this ritual, a wedding sponsor, someone from among the couple's family or friends who want to support the couple, presents the priest with a small basket or a decorated bag of coins called the "ari." The priest distributes the coins to the bride and groom who then exchange them with one another before returning them to the priest. This ritual act is intended to symbolize how the community is called to share its wealth with those in need—an act of charity that also takes

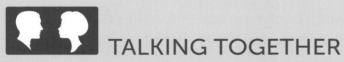

TALKING TOGETHER

- Who do you think trusts God more: poor people or rich people? Why?

- How has the economy changed since you were married? Do you remember how much your wedding cost? Looking back, are there some expenses you'd avoid if you were able to do it all over again?

- When people get upset about finances, why do they so often take it out on their spouses and children? What steps can you take to make sure that money doesn't become a reason for a family break-up?

- Despite economic uncertainty, have you been generous to appropriate charitable organizations? If you could give more to a particular one, which would it be, and what would you give? Instead of money, what else can you give?

- In many Christian communities, tithing (giving 10% of your income) is encouraged and even expected. Did you know that Catholic Church donations average less than 1% of household income? Why do you think this is the case? What should your family's contribution be?

- If you could spend more time with your spouse and children, how much time would that be? Be precise and realistic in terms of number of hours. What can be done to achieve that desire?

- Jesus looked up and saw the rich putting their gifts into the treasury, and He saw a poor widow put in two copper coins. And He said, "Truly I tell you, this poor widow has put in more than all of them, for they all contributed out of their abundance, but she out of her poverty put in all the living that she had." (Luke 21:1–4) Why do you think the old widow who gave two small copper coins was more justified than the wealthy people who gave lots of money? To which character do you relate and why?

- Would you want to win the lottery? What would you do with the money? Have you ever read stories about how winning the jackpot became a source of destruction in the winner's personal life? How do you think money can destroy lives?

place in a marriage as the spouses share what they have with one another. Then together they make offerings that contribute to the charitable works of the church.

The symbolic exchange of the *ari* is intended to remind the couple that money is not something to be hoarded. Rather, it is a gift to be shared. The very act of exchanging wealth challenges spouses to freely give all that they have to one another and to God, the "Third Person" in their marriage. It's an act of selflessness, of dependence upon God, and an affirmation of the vow, "I will love you for richer or for poorer."

Whenever I officiate a Filipino wedding that incorporates this exchange of coins, I encourage the couple to see this tradition, not as an empty ritual but as a prayer. It is a prayer for the grace to avoid the temptation of greed and the despair that can accompany possible future financial struggles, struggles that even very wealthy couples have experienced. In other words, it is a reminder to them that no one, neither rich nor poor, can put their trust in money as the key to a happy marriage.

In meeting with couples prior to marriage, I'm surprised to hear how many of them have yet to engage in a faithful discussion about financial matters. More surprising still are the large numbers of couples that, in spite of having been married for awhile, still don't know how to discuss money matters with each other in an honest, prayerful and hopeful way. All-too-often, couples struggle in their marriage due to financial problems wherein one of the spouses feels like they're alone in carrying the overwhelming burden to stay afloat.

No matter how long a couple has been married, a conversation about finances can go a long way toward improving the spouses' appreciation for each other. This particular dinnertime discussion becomes an opportunity for husbands and wives to articulate how much they are willing to invest, not in dollars and cents, but in the commitment to love and assist each other in addressing their temporal needs together.

Preparing for a healthy marriage requires a well-thought-out plan for handling future expenses together. One thing I impress upon young couples is that they first need to grow up before they attempt to grow wealthy!

Unfortunately, many younger couples today just assume that shortly after saying "I do" they'll somehow end up with a nice home, TVs in several rooms, furniture, up-to-date appliances, a well-stocked refrigerator, and spending money for vacations. In past generations, newly-married couples had far more modest expectations—starting with very little and working their way toward whatever they'd eventually have. Consider your own parents: they probably owned very little when they married but patiently worked and saved for whatever they eventually had.

In our fast-paced, fast food culture, young couples often feel pressured to build their personal kingdom in days rather than years, and sometimes they even expect to have it all in a microwavable minute!

I like to encourage couples to think of their finances metaphorically, as though their family budget is a large container that can hold a combination of large rocks and sand. The size of the container represents their total income, the rocks represent the important and necessary expenses in life (food, shelter, utilities, etc.) and the sand represents the fluffy stuff or the wants, as opposed to the needs (e.g., iPads, vacations, entertainment, etc.). If one unwisely puts sand in the container first, space for the rocks is going to be limited. Putting the rocks into the container first, however, leaves room for the sand to settle nicely into the open spaces that remain, after addressing the bigger priorities.

Responsible budgeting encourages a way for spouses to prayerfully discern together the more important expenses in their marriage, i.e., the rocks: things like insurance, education for children, reliable and sturdy appliances, and—let's not forget—charitable donations.

Giving to charities, like the ritual exchange of coins, demonstrates a couple's recognition that financial stability ultimately depends upon God's daily providence. Charitable giving is a concrete expression of a marriage built on the rock of faith, not on the shifting sands of materialistic whims.

Unfortunately, charity is frequently reduced to whatever loose change people may have in their pocket at any given moment. In our materialistic world, people give disproportionately less to charity than they spend on the miscellaneous sand, e.g., TVs, big boy toys, the latest fashions, a big house, perfectly matched furniture, and expensive vacations.

The high numbers of marital problems and divorces that are directly related to financial difficulties is another strong indication of just how important it is for couples to pray about such matters and to trust that God will provide, even when an employer's paycheck doesn't. Financial matters, like the need for more income and concerns that there is never enough, shouldn't be ignored or kept to oneself. Rather, they need to be discussed—but not in the way they're talked about in the evening news.

Let's admit it: for many of us, the almighty dollar has become God's greatest competitor. Gaining a proper perspective on family finances requires spouses to ask the simple question, "In what do we trust more, money or God?" Sacred

Scripture is very clear about how we should answer the question:

"For where your treasure is, there also will your heart be." (Matthew 6:21)

Even so, trusting in God is easier said than done, and so prayerful and humble reflection is necessary in order to honestly consider what receives the most attention in your marriage and how well this reflects the desires of a faithful heart. If we're honest, we often find that our trust in God is lacking.

Money, however, should not be considered an evil to avoid, but a gift to be understood and carefully managed. God doesn't want couples and families to be poor! In fact, God wants families to be happy and provided for generously, but it's important to understand what the real riches are in family life.

I'm always impressed when I hear people talk about how they grew up poor but didn't know it. They usually attribute their blissful ignorance to the generosity of their parents who filled their childhood home with lots of love. Families such as these are a great testimony to the fact that joyful moments of togetherness are what make for a healthy family and happy children, not big bucks spent on expensive toys. Being rich or poor is far more about one's state of mind than it is the state of one's bank account!

A teacher shared with me a great question to ponder for gaining a healthy financial perspective, "Do you live to work or do you work to live?" Think about it: if you're so busy at work that you really aren't spending quality time with your family, you're living to work and not working to live. When the priorities of one or the other of the spouses are disordered this way, it cannot help but create issues in the marriage. The old cliché is true, "Time is money," and time spent with one's spouse and one's family is the greatest investment a married person can make.

On the other hand, the idea of "working to live" needs to be clarified. Take, for example, a husband who has a job that he detests. This means that half of his life is occupied doing work that lacks a much-needed sense of personal fulfillment. In this situation, he'll naturally see the paycheck as more important than the work being done. Oftentimes, a husband and father (or wife and mother) will persist in this kind of work with the good intention of serving their family. While this can be noble, it can also border on selfishness. How? Well, employees who detest the work they're doing can very easily lose perspective and slip into caring more about the money than his or her coworkers, the boss, the customer, or even the mission of the labor.

I've met a number of very content people who left just such a job in exchange for one that may pay less but provides the best of all benefits: a great sense of personal fulfillment. These individuals often say that doing so resulted in a happier marriage, even though they may not have all of the gadgets (and headaches) of couples that have more. I can think of a number of people like this who took jobs working in church related ministries. One person I met opened a bakery and coffee shop, and another couple opened a small Christian bookstore. While these households make less money than many other couples, they have a greater sense of contentment. Their secret is that they prayerfully attained a degree of spiritual maturity that allows them to be truly grateful for what they already have, rather than giving in to the pressure our materialistic culture put on people to acquire more and more and more.

These couples have grown in faith by searching for and finding what they believe is their calling, and they answered by trusting in God to provide. They found happiness by rejecting the vicious cycle of unbridled consumerism that traps so many in our society. These couples have discovered that one can literally purchase more happiness by deciding to live more poorly, while paradoxically opening the door to living more richly than ever before.

Striking the proper balance between living to work and working to live requires a theological and prayerful approach to the topic of finances. To help find that balance, I suggest that married couples might begin by discussing how much they put in the collection basket at church.

Now before you assume that my goal is to get a donation, let me set the record straight: it isn't! I'm simply suggesting that couples can grow a great deal by considering the process they go through in determining how much to give to charity, because it reveals where their heart is, the place of true treasures.

I realize that people often feel uncomfortable when a preacher, a celebrity on a telethon, a spokesperson on a heart-tugging commercial or a homeless person asks for money. That discomfort, however, should encourage prayerful meditation about money. When a couple becomes more peaceful about how much they place in the collection basket, the poor box, or other avenues of charitable giving, it's a good indication that they're gaining a more mature understanding of money as a gift and a blessing. They're beginning, in other words, to view money more selflessly than selfishly, as less of a right and more as a privilege that brings with it certain duties.

Children obviously play a major factor in money discussions. Children are a parent's most expensive investment and most precious treasure. As a priest, I consider it a warning sign when I hear parents say that they want to provide "nothing but the best" for their children. As much as I can appreciate their genuine concern for their children, I have to point out that this way of thinking comes dangerously close to making a promise that only God can keep. The lesson is clear: The best things that parents can offer their children are lessons of virtue and unconditional love—gifts that don't cost even a single penny.

In many cases, the well-intentioned desires of a parent who wants to provide "nothing but the best" for their children unfortunately means material possessions. Showering children with expensive fashions, prestigious schools, and the latest toys and gadgets can become a selfish way for parents to reward themselves for all of their labors. Ultimately, this amounts to building the parent/child relationship on a foundation composed of material possessions or the sand we discussed earlier in this chapter.

This should prompt us to remember how Jesus cautions us not to be "like [the foolish man] who built his house on the sand." (Matthew 7:26)

History books are filled with examples of successful people who grew up without the latest fashions or the high-priced toys and who never had the opportunity to attend an impressive school. These people excelled in life because they possessed something that God wants all of us to have—a persevering spirit and the unconditional love of supportive parents.

Parents who give more attention to the rocks, the foundational things in their children's lives, realize the undeniable truth of another old cliché: Money can't buy love! Raising children with a clear sense of the difference between wants and needs builds their character, while greed destroys it. Materialism is an expensive substitute for happiness and love, and it always amounts to amassing the things that eventually render true poverty.

Limited finances admittedly create tension in the lives of many married couples, but with a devotion to prayer and a Godly perspective, any couple can experience the spiritual growth necessary to see that the most successful investment a couple can make is building a foundation on the rock of faith. That's precisely what brides and grooms promise on their wedding day: faithfulness, not material richness.

Faithful stewardship of the money you have, while approaching your financial needs with a deep trust in God, is a pathway to marital peace. The more generous you can be with those who have not, the more deeply your trust in God will grow, as will your gratitude for the many riches that are already part of your life. With this balanced perspective, your marriage will come to reflect the glorious truth that faithful spouses lead one another to the greatest wealth of all: the inheritance of the Kingdom of Heaven—the price tag of which is out of this world!

 PRAYING TOGETHER

Let us pray: Father, You are the provider of every good gift. When money and finances become difficult and confusing, help us to trust in You and to not be afraid. Lord, You know how much money we have and what we really need. Help us to keep our finances in perspective, use our money wisely, and be more generous with what we have. Give to us the courage and the strength to never let money become a source of contention between us. Help us to be good stewards and generous with our money, time, and talents. Give us insight and grace so that we can put our heart where true treasures lie—in loving You and one another. We ask this through Christ, our Savior and Lord. Amen.

 ## DINING TOGETHER

Suggested Menu: Gourmet Beef, Tofu and Grilled Veggie Quesadillas, topped with spicy sour cream. Avocado and Tomato Salad with Cilantro Citrus Oil. Dessert: Tequila and Honey Tortilla Crisps with Vanilla Ice Cream.

This menu creates an elevated fusion of flavors for a South American-inspired quesadilla. A beefy tomato and avocado gives a thick bite of freshness. The citrus tequila drizzle over sugarcoated fried tortillas takes vanilla ice cream beyond the border!

GOURMET BEEF AND TOFU
CHEESY QUESADILLAS

4 large	flour tortillas (making two quesadillas per person)
8-10 oz	top-round beef, cubed or sliced thinly
3 oz	firm tofu, cut into cubes
1 tsp	salt
1 tsp	pepper
1 tsp	garlic powder
½ tsp	ground red chili peppers
1 Tbsp	vegetable oil
½	red onion, sliced into thin strips
½	green pepper, sliced into thin strips
1 clove	garlic, finely minced
1 tsp	Worcestershire sauce
¼ cup	shredded cheddar cheese
1 can	Nonstick spray

Preheat oven to 350 degrees. Prepare a cookie sheet large enough to place two tortillas next to each other. Spray with nonstick oil.

Prepare the quesadilla filling by cutting the beef and tofu into thin equal-sized strips or cubes. Season beef and tofu with salt, pepper, garlic powder, and red chili peppers. Heat pan with oil over medium heat. Add onions, garlic, and green peppers. Sauté onions for 2–4 minutes. Remove and set aside. Add beef, and sauté for 2–4 minutes or until beef begins to brown. Add Worcestershire sauce and tofu, and gently stir together. Cook for 1–2 more minutes. Remove and set aside.

Assemble the tortillas by placing two tortillas next to each other on the cookie sheet. Distribute the sautéed vegetables and beef on each tortilla, but drain some of the juice by using a slotted spoon to scoop out the ingredients. Place vegetable and beef layers in the center of the tortilla, leaving about ½ inch from the edge of the tortilla. Sprinkle cheddar cheese on top. Place the other tortilla over the beef and vegetables, and press down lightly, careful not to have the filling spill out from the tortilla. Lightly spray the top of the tortilla with the nonstick oil. Cook in the oven for about 7–10 minutes or until the top of the tortilla begins to toast, and the cheese is completely melted. Remove and set aside for about two minutes, before cutting and plating.

Note: for instructions on spicy sour cream and plating the quesadillas, see the following recipe.

Note: if using a grill pan to cook the tortillas, turn the stove to medium low.

SPICY SOUR CREAM

½ cup	sour cream
½ tsp	garlic power
½ tsp	salt
½ tsp	pepper
½ tsp	ground red chili peppers
½ tsp	smoked paprika

Combine all ingredients in a bowl and stir together until fully incorporated. Keep refrigerated until ready to serve.

To plate the quesadillas:
Cut each quesadilla into 6 equal wedged pieces. Place on the plate in a circle, but spread apart, leaving room in the center for the salad. Dollop 1 teaspoon of sour cream atop each quesadilla wedge. Garnish with a few sprigs of fresh cilantro.

TOMATO AND AVOCADO SALAD WITH CILANTRO CITRUS OIL

2 tsp	red onion, finely minced
1	lime, juiced
1	Hass avocado, peeled, seeds removed, and diced
1 large	heirloom tomato, diced
2 tsp	fresh cilantro, chopped, plus more for garnish
1 tsp	garlic powder
1 tsp	salt
1 tsp	pepper
1 Tbsp	olive oil

Add minced onions to a bowl and add lime juice. Allow the acids of the lime juice to break down some of the strong flavors of the minced onions. Prepare the avocado by cutting it in half and carefully removing the seed. Carefully score the fruit lengthwise and cross wise, every ½ inch, creating small "cubes." Use a large serving spoon and scoop fruit into a bowl. Add the diced tomato. Season with salt, pepper, garlic powder, cilantro, and olive oil. Gently stir ingredients together. Keep chilled in the refrigerator before serving.

HONEY TORTILLA CRISPS WITH VANILLA ICE CREAM

2-3 Tbsp	regular cane sugar
2 small	flour tortillas, cut into thirds (creating 6 equally-sized nacho chips)
2 cups	vegetable oil
¼ cup	tequila
1 cup	honey
1	lime, juiced
2 scoops	Store-bought vanilla ice cream
optional	Fresh mint leaves or slice of lime for garnish

Prepare a plate with sugar, and set aside. Heat oil in frying pan. Carefully place cut tortilla chips in hot oil. When tortilla chips begin to brown, use a slotted spoon to remove tortillas, and immediately dredge in sugar, coating each side. Shake off excess sugar, and set aside. After oil cools, store in a sealed container to use for future frying.

Prepare the tequila and honey drizzle. In a small saucepan, add tequila, honey, and lime juice. Bring to light boil for about 1–2 minutes. Set aside to cool. Scoop vanilla ice cream into a bowl. Spoon some of the tequila sauce as a glaze over the ice cream. Top off with some of the crunchy sweet chips. Add a sprig of mint or a slice of lime for fresh garnish and a refreshing twist on a scoop of ice cream.

Cooking Tip:
Leftover quesadillas are best reheated by wrapping in aluminum foil and warming in a 350 degree oven for 10 minutes. This recipe can be easily modified into perfect appetizers by serving open-faced, i.e., cutting the tortillas into individual, appetizer-sized pieces and adding some of the toppings on top of each tortilla.

GROWING TOGETHER

Record some ideas, prayers, or memories about how this chapter can help strengthen your relationship.

_____
_____
_____
_____
_____
_____
_____
_____
_____
_____
_____
_____
_____
_____
_____
_____
_____
_____
_____
_____
_____
_____
_____
_____
_____
_____
_____

Chapter 10

In Sickness and In Health

The Responsibility of Loving

> " *Come, you who are blessed by my Father. Inherit the kingdom prepared for you from the foundation of the world. For I was hungry, and you gave me food, I was thirsty, and you gave me drink, a stranger and you welcomed me, naked and you clothed me, ill and you cared for me, in prison and you visited me.* "
>
> MATTHEW 25:34—36

Married life comes with many surprises, but when sickness and injury occur, it really shouldn't come as a shock to anyone. We are, after all, human.

Human beings are prone to weakness, brokenness, sickness, unhealthiness, and the general weathering of old age. I know, to some I probably sound like a rambling hypochondriac, but I'm simply speaking realistically. The word human comes from the Latin *humus*, which means "dirt" or "dust." (Ash Wednesday reminds us of this and of what we are and to what we shall return.)

Humus also happens to be the Latin root for the word "humility." In order to love one another with the profound human love that reflects the very love of God, spousal love requires great humility. Nothing humbles, tempers, and ultimately strengthens that love like sickness.

No matter how long a couple has been married, the spouses are constantly reminded of their human vulnerabilities, e.g., during the flu season, after a hard workout at the gym, or even just as fatigue takes over when playing with the children. The fact that human beings so often do get sick, experience weakness, or suffer failing health makes the promise to care for each other in "sickness and in health" an indispensable part of the wedding ceremony.

The question for couples is not so much, "What might happen if my spouse gets sick," but rather, "What will I do *when* my spouse gets sick?" God forbid that any of our loved ones should ever suffer a terminal illness or face a life-threatening injury. Surely no one invites such things. Even so, those inevitable bouts with sickness that all of us face can actually serve as a unique opportunity for spouses to deepen their love for each other.

Caring for one's spouse "in sickness" is a concrete expression of loyalty, commitment, dedication, and perseverance wherein husbands and wives can demonstrate the quality of their love for each other. God provides both the example of what it means to so love another, as well as the grace that is necessary to imitate that love, and He rewards couples according to the measure that they care for one another, most especially when they get sick.

For those living in a world that relies almost exclusively on scientific advancement as the cure-all for life's ailments, including a broken heart and a wounded spirit, approaching this delicate subject isn't always easy. It is, however, necessary, especially for married couples, if for no other reason than to remind themselves that, unless scientists can figure out how to become God, we really need to rely on the Divine Physician as our primary caregiver.

Though the Sacrament of Marriage certainly doesn't guarantee that couples will be exempt from human suffering, the sacramental grace that strengthens the spouses in fidelity to their marital covenant can alleviate some of the anxiety they might feel when considering the prospect of illness. The vows exchanged in the wedding ceremony not only promise that the spouses will be there for each other in the event of sickness, but God also promises to be there, not just for the sick person but also to give strength to the spouse who becomes the immediate caregiver. Keep in mind this isn't the case only in matters of serious illness but also when it comes to relatively minor things, like a tension headache or the common cold.

No, the sacrament doesn't mitigate the pain associated with sickness, but the recognition of God's presence working through a loving and caring spouse can certainly transform any suffering, no matter how great or how slight, into an opportunity for deeper intimacy and strengthened love.

At the wedding ceremony and at marriage counseling sessions, I have the responsibility of preaching that love doesn't always feel good. Deep love goes farther than any crush or even a deep-seated infatuation. The love between married couples establishes a covenant, a mutually self-giving promise, (not a contract), with terms and conditions inscribed deep in

TALKING TOGETHER

- Have you ever been so sick that you could not clearly express yourself? What were some of the things that brought you consolation?

- Would you consider yourself a patient person, a good listener, and a compassionate caregiver? If so, why? If not, how can you become that for your spouse?

- Have you ever discussed a Living Will with your spouse? Have you ever considered talking with a spiritual leader about the Faith implications of such a legal document?

- Why is it so hard to consider or to discuss the possibility of misfortune?

- The phrase "carpe diem" basically translates to "seize the day." Knowing that life is very fragile, how can you, as a couple, take this teaching to heart in an appropriate way for yourself and each other?

- Health is such an important part of your life and your ability to love one another. What do you do to take care of your health? Is there something that you can do together to encourage healthy longevity?

- The Scriptures show how Jesus healed the sick. How do you explain it to people when Jesus doesn't seem to heal a person you may be praying for?

- Is there a way for you to practice listening skills, compassionate concern, or care for the sick? Have you considered asking your priest, minister, or health care representative at the church for some information on how to develop this skill by getting involved in caring for sick people in your local hospital, nursing home, or homeless shelter?

the human heart, (not simply on paper). The covenant differs from a contract because God initiates and fulfills the promises that are made through human collaboration and not the other way around. In a covenant, there are no lawyers, no loopholes, and no biased judges—only faith, hope, and love.

At any stage of marriage, when the spouses look into each other's eyes, they see not only the present moment, a beautiful wife and handsome husband, but they also see the past and all that has happened from the moment they met until this very point in time. They also, however, look into the future and see hopes and dreams as yet unfulfilled, i.e., "nothing" but with a potential for "everything." A humble gaze into the future forces couples to admit that no human being can read it; that's why fortune-telling offends God, because it assumes His responsibility, replacing faith with fatalism. If couples could see into the future, given that it very well may include great tribulations, they may admit that they never would have gotten married in the first place! The unpredictability of the future gives couples these two options: fear humanity and avoid loving it, or trust God and fully embrace life and the person they love!

The prayers of the wedding ceremony encourage couples to take the proverbial leap of faith, to enter into a permanent promise vowing to protect each other from loneliness and isolation during times of sickness and vulnerability, even though they cannot perfectly protect each other from transmitting even a common cold. This part of the vow takes great faith, plain and simple!

Despite the potential pitfalls, couples promise an unconditional love founded on God's love for humanity; a Godly covenant would not have it any other way. It is this kind of love that God intends for married couples, and He promises the Grace to make it possible.

Just think about all of the bad hair days, rude comments, nitpicking and frustrating interactions with in-laws that are part of every marriage. It's enough to make a person sick to the stomach! Factor in the heartache of serious illness, and it's a wonder so many couples still continue to walk down the aisle to pledge lifelong, covenantal love. Considering all the risks, it's edifying that they do!

Taking the risk in covenantal love means willingly putting oneself in a situation that will not always be comfortable. It means knowing that in embracing one another in marriage, they are also being called to embrace the Cross of Jesus Christ. Oftentimes in married life, the Cross can entail physical or emotional sickness, and no doubt, it is a heavy cross to bear.

If one or the other of the spouses lacks the faith necessary to allow themselves to be stretched by the Cross, then the couple will inevitably experience a unique kind of suffering that, properly speaking, they inflict on each other. Not embracing the Cross in marriage opens the door to feelings of isolation, loneliness, abandonment, or separation—a predictable lack of union that stems from the fact that it is the Cross of Christ willingly embraced that makes sacramental union possible. Without the Cross, in other words, there can be no unity.

A lack of togetherness, when one of the spouses fails to carry the Cross with the other, such as in times of sickness, creates an imbalance in marriage. Loving each other only during good and healthy times is not just unrealistic, it's not even true love at all.

To realistically grow in love, couples need to learn the lessons that can only come from carrying the Cross after the example of Christ: flexibility, strength, discipline, and faithfulness. No one on Earth can avoid the Cross! It is a part of every human life, and those who attempt, in vain, to avoid it ultimately end up avoiding the real meaning of love.

True marital love, as it has been said time and again, requires sacrifice. There is no greater love than to lay down one's life for a friend! (John 15:13) No, marital love won't always feel good. However, if the burdens of human life are approached with a faith that looks beyond the mere physical, married couples can unite themselves in a profound way with the Cross of Christ, the same that brought salvation to all the world.

While we tend to think of the weight of the cross resting mainly on the person who is ill or suffering, it also puts considerable saint-making pressure on the healthy spouse who willingly provides loving comfort and care. These noble souls serve as an image of Simon of Cyrene, the man who helped Jesus carry His cross, or Veronica, the woman who wiped the face of Jesus and gave some relief to Christ on that terrible road to Calvary. In order for the healthy spouse to step up and serve the other, they must not only be physically capable but also spiritually well and courageous in charity. Thankfully, the sacramental grace given in marriage makes it possible for spouses to be saints for each other, even in the most difficult of circumstances.

The degree of sickness a spouse may be experiencing, and likewise the depth of compassion demanded of the other, obviously affects the weight of a given cross. For example, loving each other in healthy times comes quite naturally. Some couples even enjoy playing nurse for their spouse who has the sniffles. Even though it is taxing, most husbands and wives fare rather well even when their spouse endures a more major illness or operation that requires a lengthy recovery.

When health problems last an indefinite period of time, however, it's not uncommon for the healthy spouse to experience the temptation to abandon the Cross, not out of lack of love for the other, but for fear that their own life and well-being will be threatened. Dealing with a spouse's illness is difficult precisely because it demands that we no longer think of ourselves but of the other.

In a culture that simply expects comfort, many people have forgotten the art of compassion, i.e., suffering with others. While everyone has the natural instinct to pity the less fortunate, too few have developed the skills to truly serve the needs of the people they encounter. Sickness and brokenness cause us to face our own limitations, which sometimes leads us to making our own discomfort known, inadvertently or not, to the person who is suffering. In other words, because we just don't know how to help, we often make things worse.

Our world is becoming less skilled in personally dealing with sick people. This is demonstrated by the many metropolis-sized nursing homes in our culture, which unfortunately can become a city of the forgotten. Even so, it should be a comfort to know that doctors and nurses are still being trained to develop bedside manner and personal care for their patients. Priests, deacons, religious leaders, and committed lay people also undergo specific training in order to provide appropriate pastoral care to the sick. Unfortunately, couples preparing for marriage do not!

That means, many couples oftentimes have to learn this necessary discipline by hands-on experience and on-the-job training, combined with faithful prayer and hopefully the good examples of their own parents. These things can help transform a novice spouse care giver into a true "doctor of love!"

When offering counsel to couples when one of the spouses is sick, I suggest that simple things like being present, holding a hand, fluffing a pillow, or simply saying "I'm here for you" can do more for a hurting soul than the most powerful of medications. That said, the first bit of advice I always give is listen first before even attempting to fix anything.

Sickness unfortunately puts a strain on a couple's ability to communicate. Why? Sickness has its own language. The caregiver has to learn it, interpreting moans and sighs, not unlike the way parents develop an understanding of a baby's cry. In the case of illness, active listening really means hearing God's voice speaking through the suffering spouse. This is a voice that calls the spouse, as caregiver, to communicate from the heart, telling the patient in both word and deed, "I love you."

It's not always just the caregiver who needs direction, however; sometimes the person who is sick does as well. Suffering an illness doesn't excuse a person from their own marital responsibilities. Rather, it requires the humility and the honesty not to take advantage of other people's kindness. It's all too easy to milk the experience, like a crafty kid gorging on ice cream several weeks after a tonsillectomy! Remember, kindness and charity manifested through health care isn't a given, it's a gift. Loving people, like your spouse, are those modern day heroes that freely give this charity as part of the marriage covenant.

Also, some people may have a tendency to be overly dramatic at the first sign of sickness, like a hypochondriac. This leads to self-inflicted depression and can ultimately lead to theological despair. Those who are sick are called to follow Jesus' lead in the way He bore His cross—with humility and little complaint (in the Lord's case, not at all). The ill and the suffering are called to follow the Lord's example of perseverance. This means trying to get up after each fall! An active prayer life, therefore, is necessary in order to give sick people the perspective they need to carry on.

Sickness, when severe, ought to involve the compassion of professional caregivers, too. No one should feel guilty for seeking the assistance of these professionals and specialized institutions, but of course we need to remain aware that this cannot replace the one-on-one compassion that spouses promise each other.

In recent years, the world witnessed how family relationships can turn ugly in the face of great sickness, even going so far as to involve the intervention of judges and lawyers. In a controversial case involving a woman who suffered severe brain damage, a judge ordered full medical power of attorney rights to the divorced husband who sought to have her doctors remove a tube that provided water and basic nutrition. The woman eventually died from dehydration and starvation.

At one end of the battle was a divorced husband who obviously didn't want his former wife to suffer but also didn't want to deal with the challenges of caring for a sick person in his life. At the other end of the spectrum was the woman's family members who wanted her to continue receiving the most basic requirements in order to survive—water and nutrition. In the middle, was a human being—a woman broken, sick but still very much alive!

The court determined that the patient's condition placed an undue burden on the former husband, and on that day, euthanasia seemed no longer constrained by any moral boundaries. The court that originally recognized the couple's wedding vows, which included caring for the sick spouse, had chosen to invalidate and reverse its original understanding of the marriage responsibilities. The husband, who had already civilly remarried, "won" the case and received insurance money in the process. His former wife, a beloved daughter, sister, and friend, lost her life having been put to death by her former husband's decision.

Media commentators, lawyers, and religious leaders all had an opinion on this matter, and the spin on the story eventually became a hodgepodge of confusion, leaving in its wake sadness and death. How did this situation get to the point where in-laws were fighting, courts were issuing decisions on matters of morality, and the Church's teachings on the sanctity of human life were being mocked? The answer is clear: the American judicial system neither knows nor embraces the full meaning of a Christian's marital promise of fidelity in sickness. Only God can reveal what this vow really means for the couple.

In fairness, one cannot overlook the difficulty of her husband's choice, and it's not our place to judge him personally. Only God can say with certainty what he believed in his heart. Yet, observing this man's actions does say something about whether or not this marriage reflected the reality of God's intent. In the husband's mind, this woman became a very different person than the woman he originally married. She was very sick, and no doubt, her illness was a very heavy Cross to carry. Sickness however, did not take away his wife's dignity

or his responsibility to care for her. One has to wonder how a person dying by starvation and dehydration can ever be justified as dying with dignity, which summarizes the husband's argument in this case. What happened to this man's promise to be there for his wife in times of sickness? Again, this is no judgment on the man personally, but his actions; what he did and what he failed to do, in light of what he said he would do on their wedding day, are clearly two different things.

As a priest, I humbly recognize that human struggle can make it very difficult to do the right thing. Therefore, it is not my intention to make an official pronouncement on what a couple should ultimately conclude about this example. Even so, the Church does provide clear and wise direction to guide people in such difficult circumstances; it can be summed up as treating each other with dignity, in sickness and in health!

I would suggest that, if nothing else, this tragic story indicates how important it is for spouses to talk about how they would want matters handled if something like this would happen to one of them. Consider what happens if one or the other of you was unable to communicate his or her wishes? To whom would the healthy spouse turn to for guidance—the courts, lawyers, in-laws, doctors, or priests? As you might expect, I would suggest that couples listen to God, faithfully and prayerfully, trusting that He always speaks to the hearts of those who draw near to Him.

A dinner discussion about this tender issue can remind couples that God didn't offer them a lifetime of happiness and healthiness, but instead, He offers a promise of faithfulness, compassion and companionship, especially in the presence of suffering. As part of the practical aspect of this challenging discussion, couples can benefit from consultation with a spiritual leader and not just legal counsel.

This is every bit as important for newlyweds as it is couples that are celebrating a golden anniversary. In fact, every stage of marriage offers husbands and wives a unique opportunity to prayerfully consider this ever timely topic. Here are some suggestions of what married couples do well to discuss and when:

- As a newly married couple: In order to temper and purify your love early on, have a sober and serious discussion about your desires for each other, should one of you become very sick. It's a difficult conversation to have, but it's one that needs to happen, hopefully even before conceiving a child and facing what may be (Lord, forbid) a difficult and delicate pregnancy.

- After becoming parents: Encourage each other by paying attention to healthy living and by proactive sickness prevention. Make it a point to eat healthy foods, engage in regular exercise, and maintain proper social outlets, taking a holistic approach to a healthy lifestyle. Taking physical and spiritual health seriously together will give you greater assurance that you'll be up for the demands of being parents.

- After several years of marriage: It will be important for you to discuss care for your own parents who may, or already do, experience a host of health issues. Caring for parents puts a strain on young families, but it also provides an incredible opportunity to demonstrate the compassion that reaffirms and strengthens your marriage vows. It also teaches your children the importance of caring for elderly parents and fulfilling the command to "honor thy father and mother."

- As you grow older: The natural hormonal changes that come with age can strain a couple's ability to communicate. Mid-life health issues, such as menopause, a natural occurrence but a form of suffering nonetheless, requires faithful patience from both spouses, one toward the other. Persevering through these changes can be difficult, but with patient and prayerful dialogue with the Lord and one another, this can become a particularly blessed time for you to grow in closeness and in holiness.

- When the children are grown up: At this point in your marriage, you need to make it a point to stay vibrant and young-at-heart by experiencing new things, such as travel, being involved in volunteer efforts or ministerial services, or perhaps by embracing a few extra babysitting opportunities. Playing with the children or your own grandchildren can bring out the healthy childlike joy in everyone!

- In your elder years: If and when your health begins to fail as a natural part of aging, it's important to make sure that you speak honestly with one another about any physical ailments that may be present, but with hope and always avoiding complaint and the depressing language that can invite despair. In other words, as life gets harder, encourage each other with prayerful support, seeking God's grace for one another and offering gentle reminders of your love for each other. Pray together for the realization that sickness and failing health are a natural part of becoming saints, i.e., holy witnesses who bear all things with a sense of faith, hope, and love.

This practical discussion about health serves a great purpose for marriage. It can make couples more honest about their vulnerabilities, more hopeful in their weaknesses, and more faithful in their commitment to their marriage vows.

The promise to care for each other in sickness is spoken by many but prayed by few. When spouses prayerfully discuss and fulfill this marriage vow, their love expands beyond the mere human level; it substantially changes into a Godly and divine covenant love. They instill in themselves the Sacrament of Marriage as God intends it, and their love transforms the husband and wife into future saints! Saints know and live the truth that "whatever you [do] for [the least of God's people] you [do] for [God]." (Matthew 25:40)

While sickness is bound to happen, the wedding vows, if embraced with faithfulness, provide assurance to husbands and wives that God will ever remain present in their marriage, the Divine Physician who alone can give true health of body, mind, and soul.

 PRAYING TOGETHER

Let us pray: O Lord, You are the Divine Physician. You promised to be there for the sick and the suffering. When things are good and we are healthy, we sometimes put Your compassionate love on the back burner until one or the other of us suffers. When we struggle, especially with health issues, we know that there is only one place to turn—to Your merciful healing. If there is physical sickness in our marriage, teach us how to be truly compassionate. Give us grace to listen, even if we don't have the best response to give. Just give us a heart and peace of mind that tells the sick "I love you no matter what!" Jesus, You who healed so many sick people, please grant a miracle and heal our sick relatives and friends. We also pray for couples experiencing great burdens due to poor health. Give us strength so that we can help in any way possible. Give to those who are sick a sense of hope in the midst of their pain. Do not let them be tempted by discouragement, but assure them of the hope that comes from the support of Your faithful people. We ask this through Christ our Lord. Amen.

 DINING TOGETHER

Suggested Menu: Italian Seafood and Sausage Boule. Crusty dinner rolls with Herbal Whipped Spread. Dessert: Chocolate Fondue Sauce and Fresh Fruit Skewers

This romantic dinner offers a savory sausage and seafood sweetness, all in one bowl! Dining from one plate gives couples a chance to share the love. The savory sausage adds boldness to the sweet tomato broth flavors that braises fresh seafood. The herbal creamy spread over crusty bread brings texture and mellowness to the meal. The dessert, dipping fresh fruit in chocolate, makes for a happy ending—with less dishes!

SEAFOOD AND SAUSAGE BOULE

6	mussels, debearded and cleaned
4 large	scallops, cut in half
8 large	shrimp, deveined with shell removed (leave tail)
2 Tbsp	olive oil
2	Italian sausages, cut into 10-12 equal bite-sized pieces
1 clove	garlic, thinly sliced
½	white onion, finely minced
1 large	carrot, ¼" cubed
1 stalk	celery, ¼" diced
1 tsp	red pepper flakes
2 Tbsp	tomato paste
½ cup	dry white wine (substitute: ¼ cup water, ¼ cup chicken broth, 2 Tbsp lemon juice)
1 cup	seafood broth (or chicken broth)
½	lemon, juiced
½	lemon, zested
2 tsp	salt
2 tsp	black pepper
4-6 tsp	fresh parsley, minced

Clean all seafood, and keep refrigerated or sitting on top of ice, until ready to cook. Heat olive oil in a large cast iron pot over medium heat. Add sausage, and cook until slightly brown, about 1–2 minutes. Add garlic, onion, carrot, celery, and red pepper flakes, and sauté, until onions become translucent. Add the tomato paste, white wine (or substitute), broth, lemon juice, and zest, and stir together. Cook for 1–2 minutes. Add the mussels, and stir together for about 1 minute. Add the rest of the seafood, and carefully stir, making sure not to break apart the seafood. Season with salt and pepper, to taste. Cover pot, and simmer until all the mussel shells have completely opened, and the shrimp becomes pinkish white, approximately 5–7 minutes. If a mussel does not open, discard it. Turn off heat. Add the fresh parsley, and gently stir. Place in a large bowl to share.

HERBAL WHIP SPREAD:

¼ cup	cream cheese
2 tsp	sour cream
1 tsp	garlic powder
1 tsp	fresh parsley, finely minced, or ½ tsp dried
1 tsp	fresh oregano, finely minced, or ½ tsp dried
1 tsp	salt
2-4	dinner rolls, cut in half and toasted in the oven

Combine all ingredients in a bowl, and stir together until fully mixed. Use this spread over toasted crusty dinner rolls. This herbal spread offers a creamy texture to the bread that you can use to dip in the sausage and seafood sauce.

CHOCOLATE FONDUE SAUCE &
FRESH FRUIT SKEWERS

1	banana, sliced
¼	pineapple wedge, sliced
4	strawberries, rinsed with stems removed
1 cup	semi-sweet chocolate chips
¼ cup	milk
¼ cup	sweetened condensed milk
1 Tbsp	butter
	2 long skewers or long forks

Prepare all the fruit by washing, peeling, and cutting into equal bite-sized pieces. Set aside. Whisk together milk and condensed milk in a small saucepan, and heat over medium-low heat. When it begins to steam and lightly boil, turn off heat. Add the semi-sweet chocolate chips, and stir until fully melted. When fully melted, add butter, and stir together. To serve, put the chocolate sauce in a bowl, positioned at the center of a large plate. Decoratively place the fruit around the chocolate sauce. Use skewers or forks to dip the fruit in the chocolate for a romantic and delicious dessert.

Cooking Tip:
Seafood, like other proteins, requires different temperatures for cooking. Be sure to familiarize yourself with how different seafoods are prepared to get the most natural flavor out of each bite, as opposed to covering up seafood with heavy sauces.

GROWING TOGETHER

Record some ideas, memories, or prayers from this chapter that can help you strengthen your own marriage and your commitment to being effective and loving teachers for the younger generation.

_____
_____
_____
_____
_____
_____
_____
_____
_____
_____
_____
_____
_____
_____
_____
_____
_____
_____
_____
_____
_____
_____
_____
_____

Chapter 11

Mature Love

Stages of Growing Older Gracefully

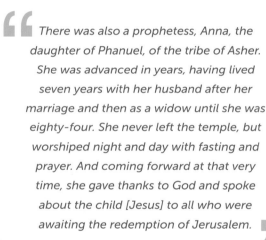

" *There was also a prophetess, Anna, the daughter of Phanuel, of the tribe of Asher. She was advanced in years, having lived seven years with her husband after her marriage and then as a widow until she was eighty-four. She never left the temple, but worshiped night and day with fasting and prayer. And coming forward at that very time, she gave thanks to God and spoke about the child [Jesus] to all who were awaiting the redemption of Jerusalem.* "

LUKE 2:36–38

During a meditation one day, I found myself asking the Lord to help me become more like a child, a strange and new prayer, at least for me. To be very honest, looking back, I have to admit that I had good reason to pray that prayer because I felt a little immature that day.

Immaturity can creep up on the best of us (including the person you vowed to love every day of your life!), and it really is amazing how often grown-ups still manage to act like spoiled children. Well, those kinds of behaviors, if not kept in check, can eventually spoil a marriage.

While immaturity is destructive, a meditation on spiritual childhood can be helpful for couples in all stages of marriage, but especially as they grow older and, hopefully, wiser. Meditating on appropriate and Godly youthfulness may bring smiles, happy memories, and great dinner conversations, but it's also a proactive reflection that can help spouses avoid unwittingly acting like babies!

Praying with a childlike heart helps couples remember what makes children so lovable. Children are so fresh! They bring a new perspective to everything, giving them a unique power to live life fully. Tapping into the joy that children have can motivate and inspire adults. For example, watching a child at play, opening gifts at Christmas, or learning how to play a game for the first time can renew the childlike joy that still resides in each of us.

Consider the bravery of a child struggling to take his first steps. In spite of numerous falls, bumps, and bruises, a child cannot be easily stopped. They'll dig down deep and do whatever it takes to accomplish their goal. Grabbing on to anything in reach that might help them remain steady, they just keep going. That is an example of true living for all of us, especially those who are getting older and who also need to hold on to things to steady their steps.

I think of a friend's daughter who was born with spina bifida. Despite her obvious physical struggles, she's enrolled in a dance class, plays soccer, and somehow manages to keep up with her big sister and big brother. She shows an indomitable spirit that makes her a force to be reckoned with! Knowing this special child's parents and extended family, I can hear them encouraging her to keep on going, no matter what. Thinking of her reminds me of life's fragility, but at the same time, I am struck by the fact that she's a glowing example of what it means to persevere. Keeping that childlike, undying spirit alive in the heart of a couple's marriage can help the spouses grow older together gracefully as God's children. All couples, but older ones in particular, really need to encourage each other to keep going, no matter what, just like my friend's daughter and her loved ones!

It's somewhat ironic, and also providential, to see the similarities between a child and an elderly person. Think about it: both walk with hesitation and with need of assistance, both sometimes have difficulty grasping complicated (and not so complicated) concepts, some face the challenge of incontinence, etc. The vulnerabilities and fragility that come with old age challenge the wild-at-heart to slow down and to live life carefully.

The images of both the baby and the senior citizen should evoke in all of us loving attention and a great respect for life. Unfortunately, however, the most fragile members of our society, the unborn and the elderly, are all-too-often the most neglected. Our utilitarian culture tends to see those who are fragile and weak as a burden rather than as an opportunity to develop the pastoral skills to meet their needs and the loving attitude necessary to embrace them in their frailty.

That kind of selfishness wreaks havoc on a marriage, but a prayerful discussion on what it means to grow old, while remaining a child of God, can help spouses to see each other's frailties (and we all have them) as an invitation to respond with the unconditional love that was promised when they took their wedding vows.

A childlike faith keeps a couple's marriage strong! Even if age slows down the activity of married seniors, an aging body cannot harm the soul. In fact, with age comes a unique kind of grace, a certain dependency on God the Father and Holy Mother Church, just as

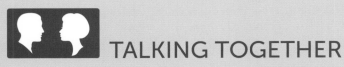

TALKING TOGETHER

- Who would you say is the sweetest elderly couple you know? What makes them so special?

- Are there characteristics that your parents have that are starting to show up in your personality and in your marriage?

- Have you ever had a conversation about how best to take care of each other when you get older? Will you ask your children for help or will you choose an assisted living situation?

- What do you think of the phenomena of families getting smaller but nursing homes getting larger and larger?

- What are some similarities and differences between a young child and an older person? Why do you think God invites us to accept faith as a child?

- Why is it so hard for young people to think about growing old but so easy for older people to want to be young?

- What are some ways that you can keep your marriage young-at-heart?

- On your wedding day, did you imagine growing older together? Did you ever talk with each other about what that looks like in your own mind, and compare it to your current reality?

a child depends on mommy and daddy. An older couple can truly become God's special children who not only need help from their own children, but especially from each other. In their humble willingness to be receptive of assistance, elderly spouses develop a deeper understanding of the true meaning of love by graciously accepting the love of another.

The modern world desperately avoids getting old. Vain attempts to discover the fountain of youth through surgeries, pills, and younger fashions for older people make it more difficult to have a fruitful discussion about getting older. The topic is almost taboo! Growing old is all-too-often portrayed as an embarrassment, which explains why so many people aren't willing to accept it gracefully.

In some cases, attempting to recapture youth has even proven dangerous, from surgeries, to medications, to all manner of crazy stunts. People have put themselves in harm's way simply because they wouldn't accept themselves for who they truly are at a certain point in life. People who do not age gracefully and avoid it kicking and screaming typically end up showing the world that they haven't grown up at all. The more they fight against the grace that comes with age, the more immature they tend to behave, literally becoming big babies!

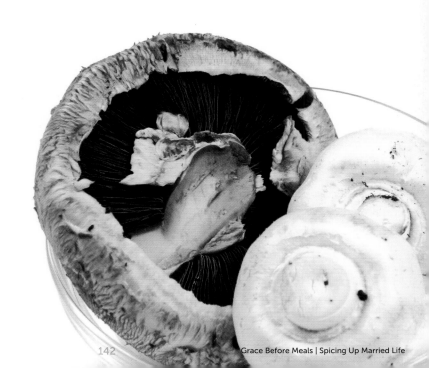

While the popular culture promotes all types of expensive ways to reclaim the look of youth, the Church sees growing older as a beautiful stage in life. That's especially true in a marriage! It is not something that should be avoided but a gift to be greeted with humility and prayer. All religions see growing older as an important stage of grace. Christians, in particular, should understand growing older as a sign of favor from God, not as a curse. That's why wedding anniversaries grow more and more meaningful with every passing year!

Consider how many things nearly everyone recognizes as improving with time—cheese, wine, the formation of diamonds, the value of antiques, etc. Clearly, not all things are better when new, and the love of a married couple is one of those things in life that gets stronger and only improves with time, with God's help, of course.

For young people, it may only take a few minutes to fall in love, but it takes many, many years to develop a true appreciation for love in its most meaningful sense. Older couples, by virtue of their experience, have an important responsibility in this regard, namely, to be a relevant and compelling witness to the fruits of commitment, perseverance, and fidelity for a generation of younger married couples who do not, as yet, possess the wisdom to fully comprehend the tremendous gifts that flow forth from marital permanence.

In marriage preparation, I invite married couples to serve as mentors for the engaged couples. I like to select couples who have been married various numbers of years in order to cover a spectrum of experience. For example, I want the engaged couples to witness the enthusiasm of recently-married couples, the stability that comes from balancing family obligations, while maintaining romance, as it exists for couples that have been married for some years, and the grace and wisdom of couples that have weathered many, many years together. While the engaged couples typically find all of the presenters interesting and helpful, they always show a particularly profound respect and awe for the older couples. Many have even told me that they were reassured and comforted by the beautiful witness of growing older together.

It's truly impressive to watch the reactions of young couples as they listen to the advice of loving older couples. It calls to mind the image of a child hearing a fairytale come to life! Oftentimes the young lovers look into the future and wonder (and hopefully pray) that their marriage will endure and be just as blessed in their future years.

As a priest, I've felt that same awe and admiration for more senior couples, too. When I celebrate the renewal of vows for golden wedding anniversaries, there are more tears of joy and hopeful emotion than on the wedding day fifty years before! Those anniversary celebrations prove that covenant love is real! Despite the struggles that are part of every relationship, these special couples show that they love each other just as much, if not more, on their anniversary than they did on their wedding day. What an inspiration for all of us!

In the Catholic wedding ritual, the priest prays a blessing over the couple after they've exchanged vows: a nuptial blessing that asks God to give the newly-married couple the grace to grow old together. While the newlyweds may have difficulty thinking of future events beyond their wedding reception, the purpose and effect of this sacred prayer cannot go unnoticed. God, who sees their lives and their love outside of time, envisions these young people as His children, and He will continue to see them this way, no matter how old they get. God's plan for marriage as expressed in this prayer lets everyone present know that the Lord wants more for this couple than to simply maintain the love they already have. Rather, He wills that they should grow ever more deeply in love with each other over the course of time. In other words, He wants their puppy love to grow into eternity!

At this point, I'd like to offer some pastoral suggestions specific to couples at particular stages of married life.

Younger Couples

The next time you go to church, take a look around, and see if there are any older couples in the congregation that you see regularly. Pray for them. Get to know them. One of these days, simply tell these older couples how their faithfulness to God and each other is inspiring to you.

Middle-Aged Couples

While that term "middle age" has become rather subjective in our day and age, you know who you are! Take a moment to prayerfully consider whether or not your life together truly reflects the gracefulness of your age. Ask yourself, "Do we maintain a young-at-heart attitude, without simply trying to be 'young and hip,' which only makes young people feel awkward?" At this stage of married life, couples should have good friendships with other couples that have been married about that same number of years— people who support one another in matters of faith, study, civic involvement, and societal improvement. In other words, you're at a stage in your lives where you can impact society for the good through your professional careers and by your witness as a mature couple. Do you?

Older Couples

By this stage in life, you either have a tendency toward being sweet or being grouchy! (Sorry for the stereotype, but you have to admit that caricature makes for great plots for movies and sitcoms!) Whatever your particular attitude as an older couple happens to be, it didn't just develop overnight. Rather, it's the result of daily decisions made over the course of many years about how you choose to look at the world, each other, and your relationship with God. That being said, it's never too late to seek the grace to look at the world anew through the eyes of faith, to recapture, if necessary, the childlike joy that still resides deep within your heart. At this stage in married life, it's important to embrace the fact that you're in a unique position to provide a great witness to the world by staying as active as possible, serving as a source of comfort and hope simply by being joyful.

In conclusion, when couples prayerfully take the time to reclaim a healthy understanding of what it means to be God's children, no matter how old they may be, they are well on their way to maturing gracefully (i.e., full of grace), and they will inspire the young couples in their lives by their example of faithfulness and love!

As I prayed for the Lord to help me be more like a child, I thought of my grandparents and my parents. I meditated on what they might have been like as children, how they grew up, what is was like for them when they fell in love and got married, and where they are in their lives today. I felt moved to pray for married couples everywhere, at all stages of marriage, and I reflected on the fact that faithfulness does not come easily.

I then contemplated St. Augustine's description of God as "ever ancient, ever new" and how God's faithfulness to His people throughout the entirety of their lives can help us by example to remain faithful to each other and to the promises we have made.

By God's Grace, I uttered a prayer that I think can help all couples at all stages of marriage: "Lord, help me to be an old dog that can learn new tricks!"

Married couples: Tweak this prayer as you see fit and reflect on it. Of course, love is not a trick to be played on each other, but this prayer, in spite of its playful tone, or perhaps because of it, reminds us that loving one another in marriage is a matter of living faithfully as a child of God. No matter how young or how old you may be, exercise the will to live each and every day of your marriage with an open heart, willing to learn new ways to love God, to love life, and to love one another more deeply and more faithfully than the previous day.

Remember, from couples who are young urban professionals just starting out, to couples who are senior citizens enjoying their retirement years, all are God's children. Pray, therefore, for the grace to always see your spouse as a child of God, that you may learn to love as He does, recognizing in humility that we, too, are but beautiful children in His sight!

 # PRAYING TOGETHER

Let us pray: Father, "Ever Ancient and Ever New," You see us as Your children, even though we don't always remember that spiritual reality. We may feel the fragility of our years, or we sometimes feel shame, because we act more like spoiled babies, rather than act with dignity. When we consider our marriage, we know that we are called to help each other in life's journey, as a parent would help a child walk or as a cane keeps us upright. Help us to become a source of true help to each other. Help us, that together we may grow older and wiser in grace. Help us to look back at our younger years with thankfulness and not with an unhealthy longing for the past. Father, we pray for those older couples that may feel alone or abandoned by their children and are left to grow old without the help they need. We pray for those people that care for the aged and infirm. May those workers treat the residents with compassion, caring for them as treasure chests that contain much wisdom, experience and dedication to life. Father, help couples to be young-at-heart, willing to learn and experience as much as life provides, while being content with the reality of slowing down in this busy world. And Father, help all couples to be as beautiful as the leaves of a tree, which although ready to fall to the ground, give radiance, brilliance and color to a fall day. You, Lord of all the ages, have a plan for each moment of our lives. Help us to trust that You are with us, and all married couples, as we grow older in grace, through Christ our Lord. Amen.

 # DINING TOGETHER

Suggested Menu: Oven-fried Portabella Mushroom Steaks, Sweet and Savory Zucchini and Squash Hash, and Herbal Couscous. Dessert: Passion Fruit Mousse

Vegetables prepared in savory and textured ways can make for a romantic and healthy meal! Meaty mushrooms can satisfy even picky beefsteak lovers. The squash and zucchini hash, glazed with tartness and sweetness from raisins, adds a rich and bright flavor to this menu. The couscous provides great herbal flavors to round out the meal. For dessert, indulge in an easy white chocolate passion fruit mousse that definitely helps couples celebrate.

OVEN FRIED PORTABELLA STEAKS

2 large	portabella mushrooms, cleaned with stems removed
1 cup	all-purpose flour
2	eggs beaten with 2 Tbsp of water
1 cup	Italian seasoned bread crumbs
4 Tbsp	olive oil
2 tsp	salt
2 tsp	pepper
1 can	Nonstick spray

Preheat oven to 350 degrees, and apply nonstick spray to a sheet pan. Carefully remove mushroom stem, with a small paring knife. Prepare one dish of flour for dredging, one dish for the egg and water combination, and one dish for the breadcrumbs. Gently rinse mushroom under cold water, and immediately dredge in flour, until all sides are coated. Move mushrooms to the egg and water combination, and soak until the mushrooms are covered in egg. Transfer mushrooms to coat all sides with the Italian seasoned breadcrumbs. Heat olive oil in a frying pan. Sear mushroom for 1–2 minutes on each side. Remove and place on a sheet pan, and immediately sprinkle with salt and pepper. Put mushrooms in the oven for 8–10 minutes. Mushrooms should have crunchy exterior but be soft to the touch. Remove and let mushrooms rest a few minutes, before cutting and serving.

SWEET AND SAVORY ZUCCHINI AND SQUASH HASH

1 Tbsp	olive oil
1 cup	zucchini, diced
1 cup	yellow squash, diced
1	garlic clove, finely minced
1 pinch	red-hot chili pepper flakes
1 Tbsp	fresh parsley, minced
½	red onion, finely minced
¼ cup	dried raisins or cranberry raisins
2 Tbsp	pine nuts (substitute: chopped walnuts)
1-2 Tbsp	white vinegar
1 tsp	salt
½ tsp	pepper

Heat 1 tablespoon of olive oil in a large nonstick pan over medium-high heat. Add zucchini, squash, garlic, pepper flakes, parsley, onion, pine nuts, and raisins. Sauté for 2–4 minutes. Deglaze pan by adding the white vinegar and gently stirring together. Season with salt and pepper, to taste.

Note: for presentation, use a ring mold to plate.

HERBAL COUSCOUS

1 cup	uncooked couscous
2 cups	water
2 tsp	butter
½ tsp	garlic powder
½ tsp	dried oregano
½ tsp	dried parsley
½ tsp	dried thyme
optional	salt and pepper

Boil water in a large saucepan. When water comes to a rolling boil, add couscous, and stir and cook for about 7–10 minutes or until soft. Turn off heat. Add butter and all other ingredients. Stir together. Add salt and pepper to taste.

PASSION FRUIT WHITE CHOCOLATE MOUSSE

¼ cup   milk

2 Tbsp   passion fruit puree
(substitute: your favorite choice of fruity jam)

1 Tbsp   unsalted butter

2 Tbsp   sugar

½ cup   semi-sweet white chocolate chips

2   eggs, yolks separated from whites

2 cups   heavy whipping cream,
whipped to soft peaks

Small pot of boiling water with a heat-resistant bowl on top of it, and two bowls chilled in the freezer.

Prepare a double-boiler by placing a nonreactive heat-resistant bowl over a small pot of boiling water. Add milk, fruit puree (or jam substitute), butter, sugar, and white chocolate, and stir until chocolate chips have melted completely and ingredients are fully incorporated with the fruit. Turn off heat, and add 2 egg yolks, and quickly whisk together until creamy. Set aside. In a separate bowl that has been chilled in the freezer, use a hand blender to whip the cream, until it develops soft peaks. In another separately chilled bowl, whip the egg whites, until thick and fluffy. Gently combine the whipped cream and whipped egg whites with the fruit and chocolate sauce in a large bowl. Gently fold all ingredients together, until ingredients are fully incorporated, and the color of the puree or jam substitute is evenly mixed. Chill the mousse in the freezer for about one hour or until the mousse becomes firm, but not frozen. Store in the refrigerator after it has set and become firm. To serve, use an ice cream scoop or spoon into a martini class, and garnish with a sprig of fresh mint.

Cooking Tip:
Making mousse can be very difficult, because of proportions and temperature. In order to get the fluffiest whipped cream and egg whites, be sure to keep your mixing bowls very chilled!

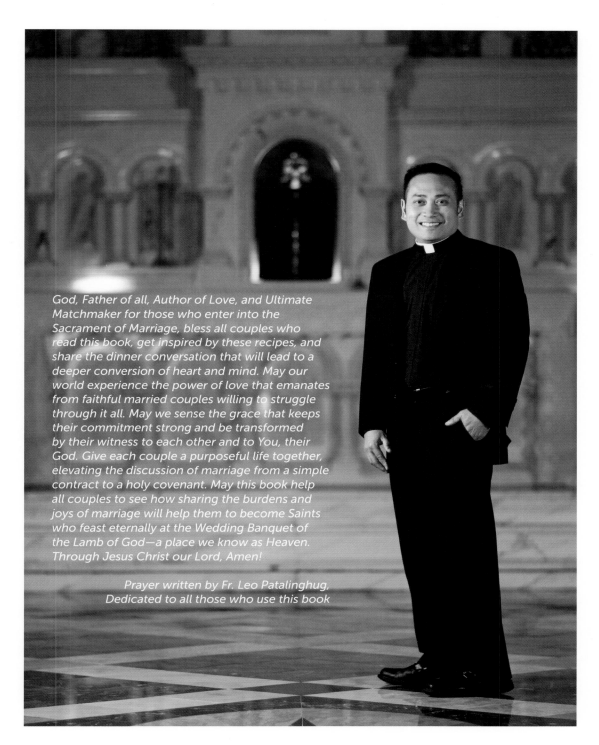

God, Father of all, Author of Love, and Ultimate Matchmaker for those who enter into the Sacrament of Marriage, bless all couples who read this book, get inspired by these recipes, and share the dinner conversation that will lead to a deeper conversion of heart and mind. May our world experience the power of love that emanates from faithful married couples willing to struggle through it all. May we sense the grace that keeps their commitment strong and be transformed by their witness to each other and to You, their God. Give each couple a purposeful life together, elevating the discussion of marriage from a simple contract to a holy covenant. May this book help all couples to see how sharing the burdens and joys of marriage will help them to become Saints who feast eternally at the Wedding Banquet of the Lamb of God—a place we know as Heaven. Through Jesus Christ our Lord, Amen!

*Prayer written by Fr. Leo Patalinghug,
Dedicated to all those who use this book*

GROWING TOGETHER

Record some of your ideas, memories, or prayers about how this chapter can help strengthen your marriage.

_____

_____

_____

_____

_____

_____

_____

_____

_____

_____

_____

_____

_____

_____

_____

_____

_____

_____

_____

_____

_____

_____

_____

_____

_____

_____

Chapter 12

'Til Death Do Us Part

Reaching the Finish Line

Be subordinate to one another out of reverence for Christ. Wives should be subordinate to their husbands as to the Lord. For the husband is the head of his wife just as Christ is head of the Church, he, himself, the savior of the body... Husbands, love your wives, even as Christ loved the Church and handed himself over for her to sanctify her, cleansing her by the bath of water with the word, that he might present himself the church in splendor... He who loves his wife loves himself... we are members of His body... this is the great mystery, but I speak in reference to Christ and the church. ❞

EPHESIANS 5: 21–23, 25, 28, 30, 32

You may have heard the old saying, "Marriage is not a sprint; it's a marathon." Well, it may be a cliché, but that's only because it's so true!

Surviving a marathon requires great determination, training, strength, and most importantly, an unbeatable desire to cross the finish line. As any long-distance runner can tell you, there's great joy in crossing that painted white line on the road, whether you're the very first one to do so or even if you're the very last. With something as arduous as a marathon, simply crossing the finish line is winning. This is true for marriage as well.

But what exactly is the finish line in marriage? Is it a milestone anniversary? Is it the purchase of the perfect retirement home or maybe just saving up enough money to comfortably enjoy your senior years?

Some individuals are so lacking in ardor and strength that they don't even stay in the race, and others approach marriage with a sprinter's mentality, as though much will be achieved quickly, immediately, and even instantly. For those who think that way, the only "finish line" they're likely to cross is the end of a marriage.

Clearly, the marriage journey is traveled on a course that has many twists and turns, not to mention more than a few dangerous potholes. Reaching the finish line will entail meeting many challenges head-on, right from the very start. Rest assured, marriage athletes, there is hope!

God's Grace comes to those who strive to reach the finish line together.

Remember the unique prayer you said on your wedding day, "I will love you always, until death do us part"?

I know that for many couples, whether newly engaged or married many years, a discussion about death and dying is taboo. Without a strong sense of religious faith, the entire concept of death can be frightening to a couple. They may view death as the unavoidable reality that will one day bring not only life but their love to a tragic end, and so they avoid the topic at all costs.

The faithful Christian, on the other hand, knows that life doesn't end with death; it merely changes. Furthermore, for a married couple, we know that death does not put an end to love; it simply changes it from a temporary love into an eternal one. When counseling a grieving spouse, I often try to help them understand how the "eyes of faith" can help us to see the death of a loved one, not just as a loss, but as an opportunity to increase our spiritual love for that person.

Just ask my grandmother who, after 70 years of marriage, still continues to "talk" with my grandpa in prayer, even though they are now separated from one another by death. My grandparents' love for each other has endured in a spiritual way, and my grandpa is even closer to my grandma's heart and soul than ever. Don't misunderstand, she misses him terribly, but continuing their love in a spiritual way, while remembering the life they shared when he was on Earth, brings her great consolation.

In fact, my entire family can still feel grandpa's presence at every gathering, especially when we gather in prayer. While he is not here with us, our love for him remains in our hearts forever. Death cannot take that away. Don't just take it from me; believe St. Paul who said, "If there are prophecies, they will be brought to nothing; if tongues, they will cease; if knowledge, it will be brought to nothing... Love never fails." (1 Cor. 13:8)

While death often brings great confusion about the meaning of life and love, faithful Christians, imbued with the theological virtue of hope, are called to look beyond their pain to seek the inspiration and grace necessary to live their own lives even better—more fully, more faithfully, and more focused on getting to Heaven.

 ## TALKING TOGETHER

- Why is a discussion of "until death do us part" so often avoided by couples, especially young couples? How can this challenging topic be better discussed during marriage preparation and in prayer with one another?

- Do you know a widow who you think should remarry? How do you think this new relationship would be received by surviving children and in-laws? Have you ever discussed what you would want the other person to do after a spouse dies?

- What are some things your spouse does for you that will help you get to Heaven? Are there some things you do that may be impeding your spouse from reaching Heaven?

- Have you ever read about the inspiring life of Saint Gianna Molla? How do you inspire your children to become saints? Are you seeking to become a saint yourself?

- Do you pray for your spouse throughout the day? Have you ever shared your personal prayer for each other? How can prayer make you more connected to each other in this marriage?

- What do you think Heaven is like? Do you know what Scripture says about Heaven? How can these images of Heaven relate to your life now?

- Have you ever met a person who lost a loved one and seems to have died with him or her? What advice would you give to encourage that person to live fully?

- Read the story at the end of the chapter. What do you think about the woman who finished a marathon at 92 years old? How can your marriage learn from the dedication of this woman?

Grieving the loss of a spouse is a particularly heavy cross to bear, but fidelity urges the surviving spouse to continue moving on with life, knowing that the finish line beckons. Once again, I think of my grandma who now lives her life with a renewed focus on her Heavenly destination, because she firmly believes that my grandpa and Our Lord are awaiting her there. She simply must continue that race!

Yes, getting to Heaven *is* the finish line, and those who make it will, at long last, get to celebrate their glorious finish with the Saints, that "great cloud of witnesses" that have been spurring them on all the while!

In marriage preparation sessions, I like to challenge couples with the Scripture passage found at the beginning of this chapter—an exhortation from St. Paul that can cause great anxiety to people who live in a society, such as ours, that has an unhealthy attachment to individualism. In fact, it's not uncommon for the bride-to-be to voice her concern that the Apostle's words sound misogynistic.

I often have to remind couples that Sacred Scripture is God's Word, and we can therefore be confident that St. Paul isn't telling us to treat women unfairly! This being the case, we must resist the temptation to disregard (or worse, to reject) St. Paul's words, as though they are simply "outdated," and instead seek to understand what he (and the Lord!) is trying to tell us.

A more accurate interpretation of this text indicates that spouses are being encouraged by St. Paul to recognize how inseparable they truly are, like a single body with different parts that are working together in harmony toward a common goal: namely, crossing the finish line to Heaven.

Marriage, according to St. Paul, reflects the love between Christ (the Bridegroom) and His Mystical Body on Earth, the Church (His Bride), a relationship that thrives on the Bridegroom's self-donating, sacrificial love and the humble receptivity of His Bride. Bearing this in mind, we should see in this exhortation a poignant description of the kind of collaboration demanded of husbands and wives who are likewise called to work together as one unified body on a journey to Heavenly perfection!

When couples are truly and faithfully working together, St. Paul's admonition makes perfect sense! He challenges couples to ask: Does our marriage look like a body with two heads running in different directions, or does it resemble St. Paul's concept of one body made of different parts, each respecting the other's unique roles while working toward the same goal?

Staying focused on the goal of marriage and getting each other to Heaven helps spouses approach their temporal responsibilities, needs, and desires with a healthy sense of perspective. Yes, gold rings, romantic vacations, and a comfortable retirement home can provide some joy and perhaps even a sense of stability. But couples who focus on their spiritual goals are more prone to rejoice in what they already have, as opposed to worrying about what they don't have and perhaps don't really need. When a marriage is grounded in faith, in other words, the husband and wife recognize in each other the great treasure they discovered the day they met: A spouse who will help them reach Heaven, the place where love reaches a state of eternal perfection.

Jesus reminds us, "Love one another as I have loved you" (John 15:12). And how did Jesus love us?

With a spousal love for His Bride the Church, Jesus opened for us the way to Heaven (in fact, He is the Way!). His saving work continues even now as He aids us by Grace on the journey of faith that we might one day come to share in His glory for all eternity. This is the kind of love that God has for His people, and it should be the same type of love that married people have for each other.

As mentioned in previous chapters, marriage is a sign of the union between God and man, between Heaven and Earth. It's a reminder that life on Earth, although imperfect and filled with trials, is ordered toward Heaven. When couples lose this perspective and give each other grief and hell, in what direction do you think they are taking their marriage? Patience, charity, forgiveness, and love toward one another, on the other hand, are all measures of a faithful marriage (notice I didn't say perfect marriage) and one that reflects the desire to enter Heaven. Such couples not only bring a little bit of Heaven into their marriages in the here-and-now, they also bring by way of their example a little bit of Heaven to our world.

Living your marriage well, exercising sexual fidelity, raising and educating children, and providing the appropriate intimacy for each other, helps bestow sanctity (i.e., saintliness) upon a marriage.

Consider, for example, the life of Dr. Gianna Molla, an Italian pediatrician who died on April 28, 1962. Gianna was a loving wife, dedicated mother, and faithful Catholic who was canonized by Pope John Paul II on May 16, 2004, not because she was a member of a religious order or because she was a "mover and shaker" in the Church but because she lived an ordinary life extraordinarily.

As a physician working in Milan, St. Gianna considered herself a missionary in the medical field doing everything in life with a gaze firmly fixed on Heaven as her final goal. By her faithfulness to the teachings of the Church and her tireless efforts to console the sick and to bring hope to the dying, she inspired many others to seek and to find the path to Heaven as well.

As a young woman, Gianna was diagnosed with a medical condition that promised not only to complicate her pregnancies but to pose a serious threat to her health as well. With sincere faith and trust in God, however, she and her husband refused to use contraception and agreed to cooperate with God in bringing children into the world, in spite of the suffering they knew it would entail.

When the couple conceived their second child, the medical complications were so severe that they threatened Gianna's life. Her doctor recommended that she have an abortion, but in her mind there was no question that the best thing to do was to sacrifice herself so that her child could live. Knowing the risks, Gianna chose to embrace the demands of true love, and after much suffering she gave birth to the couple's third daughter, Gianna Emanuela, on Good Friday, 1962.

Seven days later, her husband, Pietro, and their children said goodbye to the wife and mother who willingly sacrificed herself so that her child could live. In doing so, St. Gianna Molla put an exclamation point on her magnificent example of faithful marriage as she triumphantly made her way to life's finish line: Heaven.

To all such heroic people, Heaven's door opens! St. Gianna exhibited heroic fidelity in her marriage, bore powerful witness to the sanctity of human life, and showed unshakable hope in the midst of personal suffering, all for the sake of her children!

Present at the canonization Mass for St. Gianna Molla was her husband and all of her children. Can you imagine the deep sense of love that filled their hearts for her? They love her not only as a wife and a mother but as a Saint! Her husband, through his own courage and faithfulness to the vows they professed on their wedding day, played no small role in helping Gianna get to Heaven. Now she, in turn, is able to help him and her children arrive at that same finish line, through her prayerful intercession.

While this incredible love story fills us with inspiration, it also leads us to other important questions about the death of a spouse. Many may ask, "Is it okay to date someone else or remarry if your spouse dies?" The answer from the Church (and Sacred Scripture) is "yes," because the vow "until death do us part" has been fulfilled.

In Her wisdom, the Church provides special preparatory exercises to make sure that marriage among remarrying widows and widowers is done with great pastoral attention and care, providing a number of insightful questions for couples to discuss such as: If you have children, how are they likely to react to this new relationship? How will you integrate your departed spouse's love within the love you now share with your future spouse? How will your future husband or wife encourage (or discourage) you in keeping the memories of your former spouse alive?

Parting in death fulfills a marriage rather than ending it. This marks the beginning of a new stage in the marriage. In fact, it encourages the surviving spouse to persevere in running toward the finish line with gusto! For some, this will include remarrying, for others, it will include, well, simply running. Literally!

In the 2010 Honolulu Marathon, 92-year-old Gladys Burrill, a great-grandmother and widow, demonstrated the power of love when she completed the 24-mile trek across the island. A woman on a mission, Gladys had dedicated this race to her husband of 69 years, Eugene, who had died just days before she attempted the same marathon in 2008. Unable to finish that year and the next due to illness, Gladys approached the race in 2010 with the memory of Eugene spurring her on to continue living her life to the fullest.

With just 200 yards to go, Gladys was struggling and unsure that she would be able to reach the finish line. Just then, Hall of Fame marathon runner Jimmy Muindi of Kenya rushed out to meet her on the course and, like a messenger sent from Heaven, he encouraged Gladys to trust in God. After the race, Gladys told reporters that the message was "so precious" that it renewed her energy. Shortly thereafter, Gladys crossed the finish line with joy, gratitude, prayer, and of course her memory of her husband.

Living life fully always means living life in the direction of Heaven, and living life in the direction of Heaven in marriage means faithfully seeking God's Grace, in order to lead one's spouse to everlasting life in the Divine presence where the celebration never ends. After crossing this finish line, we know that the crown of eternal glory awaits us, as well as a crowd of Angels and Saints to cheer our victory.

Those who make it will encounter their spouse once again, as well as all who have gone before us marked with the sign of faith. At this point, the point where life really begins, we will also find God, the One who promises to love us forever.

Doesn't God's promise to the couple sound strikingly familiar to the promise you made to your spouse on your wedding day?

 ## PRAYING TOGETHER

Let us pray: Lord of Life, we pray for Your help in crossing the finish line. We pray that we, as one body, will work together for that common goal. Help us to always encourage each other. If we ever become a stumbling block for each other, give us the strength and the grace to ask for forgiveness from You and from one another. Lord, many things seem to keep us distracted from our most important obligations in life. Therefore, help us to be humble and obedient to Your Church's teachings about the sanctity of our marital responsibilities, so we can be for others what You ask us to be: living witnesses of Your unchanging love. May each day be an "I Do"—a renewal of our spousal love, so when God invites us to that eternal wedding banquet, we may be ready and spiritually able to accept this invitation to celebrate forever! With the prayers of all the angels and saints, especially St. Joseph and the Blessed Virgin Mary and all saintly married couples, we ask this through Christ our Lord. Amen.

 # DINING TOGETHER

Suggested Menu: Pan-seared Chicken Tender "Frances" with a white wine, lemon, and caper sauce. Side of Balsamic Beans and Seasoned Steamed Potatoes. Dessert: Graham-crusted Banana Split.

This menu elevates children's meals to a whole new level! Chicken tenders get seasoned with a French-styled sauce. Typical potatoes and beans get splashed with balsamic vinegar. And banana splits receive a makeover with sautéed graham crusts and fresh berry compote.

CHICKEN TENDER "FRANCES"

6-8	chicken tenders (3-4 per person)
1 tsp	salt
1 tsp	pepper
1 cup	all-purpose flour, separated
2 Tbsp	olive oil
1 Tbsp	butter
½ cup	dry white wine (substitute: ¼ cup of chicken stock with 1 Tbsp lemon juice)
1 cup	chicken stock
1 Tbsp	yellow mustard
4 slices	lemons, seeds removed
2 Tbsp	capers with the juice

Season chicken tenders with salt and pepper. Dredge in flour, and set aside. Reserve 1 teaspoon of flour. Discard the rest of the flour. Heat olive oil and butter in a large nonstick sauté pan over medium heat. When butter is completely melted and oil is hot, carefully place chicken tenders in hot oil, keeping each tender separated and not overcrowding the pan. Depending on the size of the pan, it may be necessary to cook chicken in batches of 3–4 at a time. Cook each side for 3–4 minutes or until each side is golden brown. Once both sides have cooked, remove from heat and set aside. Add 1 teaspoon of all-purpose flour to the hot pan, and whisk together. Add white wine (or substitute), chicken stock, and mustard, and whisk together. Add lemon slices and capers, and stir together. Return the chicken to the sauce, and continue to cook for 3–5 more minutes.

BALSAMIC BEANS AND SEASONED STEAMED POTATOES

½ cup	water
1 cup	baby red skinned potatoes, quartered to make 1" cubes or strips
1 Tbsp	olive oil
1 Tbsp	butter
1 clove	garlic, finely minced
8-10 oz	string beans, ends trimmed, cut into ½" pieces
1 Tbsp	balsamic vinegar
½ tsp	salt
½ tsp	pepper

Put ½ cup of water in a frying pan with potatoes over medium heat. When water is almost evaporated, reduce to low heat, and add olive oil and butter to the pan. Add garlic, and sauté for 1–2 minutes. Add beans and cook until they turn bright green, 1–2 minutes. Turn off heat. Add balsamic vinegar, salt, and pepper.

GRAHAM CRUSTED BANANA SPLIT

2	bananas, peeled and cut into four equal pieces
½ cup	graham crackers, ground in a food processor
1 tsp	butter
2 tsp	lemon juice
1-2 tsp	sugar
2 cups	any berry combination: strawberries, blueberries, raspberries, cherries
2 scoops	store-bought vanilla ice cream
optional	whipped cream
optional	sprig of fresh mint for garnish
optional	chopped walnuts

Put crushed graham cracker crumbs on a plate. Roll the cut bananas onto the cracker crumbs, coating all sides of the banana. Heat butter in a small sauté pan. When butter is melted, add the bananas, and sauté on all sides of the banana until golden brown. Remove and set aside.
In the same pan, add lemon juice, sugar and berries. Sauté until juice are released. To plate, scoop ice cream into a deep bowl. Decoratively place bananas on top of the ice cream. Scoop some of the berries and some of the natural juices on top of the banana or around the ice cream.

Option: Add a dollop of optional whipped cream to finish the dessert, with a sprig of mint, a light sprinkle of any remaining graham crackers and optional chopped walnuts.

Cooking Tip:

The wine you cook with is the best type of wine to serve at dinner. Getting smaller bottles of wine or using boxed wine that remains in your refrigerator helps with cost, because it helps you to control the amount of wine used for cooking as opposed for drinking! In other words, if a couple can share one bottle of wine between the two of them, then make sure you have some less expensive boxed wine or smaller bottles of wine on hand for cooking!

GROWING TOGETHER

Record some of your ideas, memories or prayers about how this chapter can help strengthen your marriage.

_____

_____

_____

_____

_____

_____

_____

_____

_____

_____

_____

_____

_____

_____

_____

_____

_____

_____

_____

_____

_____

_____

_____

_____

Recipe Index
Arranged Alphabetically

Metric Conversion Chart

Liquids

U.S.		IMPERIAL		METRIC	
1	teaspoon	⅙	fluid ounce	5	milliliters
1	tablespoon	½	fluid ounce	15	milliliters
⅛	cup	1	fluid ounce	30	milliliters
¼	cup	2	fluid ounces	60	milliliters
½	cup	4	fluid ounces	120	milliliters
¾	cup	6	fluid ounces	180	milliliters
1	cup	8	fluid ounces	240	milliliters
1	pint (2 cups)	16	fluid ounces	470	milliliters
1	quart (4 cups)	32	fluid ounces	950	milliliters
1	gallon (4 quarts)	128	fluid ounces	3.8	liters

Oven Temperatures

TYPE OF HEAT	°FAHRENHEIT	°CELCIUS
very low	225	107
	250	121
low	275	135
	300	148
moderate	325	162
	350	176
moderately high	375	190
	400	204
high	425	218
	450	232
very high	475	246